MODERN HEROES OF THE CHURCH

MODERN HEROES OF THE CHURCH

LEO KNOWLES

Our Sunday Visitor Publishing Division
Our Sunday Visitor, Inc.
Huntington, Indiana 46750

Our Sunday Visitor Publishing Division
Our Sunday Visitor, Inc.
200 Noll Plaza
Huntington, IN 46750

ISBN: 1-931709-46-7 (Inventory No. T27)
LCCN: 2002113413

Cover design by Tyler Ottinger
Interior design by Sherri L. Hoffman

PRINTED IN THE UNITED STATES OF AMERICA

Foreword

❧

*I*n accordance with the decrees of Pope Urban VIII, the author and publisher wish to state that nothing in these pages is intended to anticipate any future decision of the Holy See.

In addition to the sources listed in the bibliography, much of the material for *Modern Heroes of the Church* was researched from Internet websites.

Chapter Three appeared originally as an article in *Our Sunday Visitor,* and Chapter Fifteen as an article in *Catholic Digest.*

Several other chapters, now updated, appeared in my book *Candidates For Sainthood* (Carillon Books, 1978).

Contents

1. "Should I Be a Nazi — or a Catholic?"   9
   Franz Jägerstätter

2. "Come Sweet Death on Wednesday"   15
   John Bradburne

3. "I Saw Jesus Moving through the World"   25
   Venerable Marthe Robin

4. "Avoid Everything Half-Done"   29
   Venerable Edel Quinn

5. "Dying Is a Full-Time Job"   38
   Father Vincent McNabb, O.P.

6. "I Have Promises to Keep"   48
   Dr. Tom Dooley

7. "It Is Constancy That God Wants"   67
   Venerable Matt Talbot

8. "Don't Stop Praying"   75
   Blessed Brother André

9. "Where I Sow, Others Will Reap"   86
   Venerable Charles de Foucauld

10. "Christ Streamed Out upon Me"   104
    Saint Edith Stein

11. "My Reign Will Be a Short One"   114
    Pope John Paul I

12. "I Cannot Risk Losing God" 127
Saint Josephine Bakhita

13. "We Are Prophets of a Future Not Our Own" 137
Archbishop Oscar Romero

14. "We Do Very Little Good When We Embark on Our Own" 152
Blessed Cyprian Tansi

15. "In Five Hours I Shall See Jesus" 161
Jacques Fesch

16. "We Have a Job to Do" 167
Cardinal Basil Hume

17. "A Life Lived in the Full Sense of the Word" 173
Blessed Luigi Beltrame Quattrocchi and Blessed Maria Corsini

18. "I Am the Happiest Man on the Face of the Earth" 177
Father Mychal Judge, O.F.M.

Bibliography 183

1

"SHOULD I BE A NAZI — OR A CATHOLIC?"

Franz Jägerstätter

On the afternoon of August 9, 1943, a young Austrian farmer named Franz Jägerstätter waited calmly in his cell at Berlin's Brandenburg Prison for the escort that would take him to the guillotine nearby. On the table beside him lay a paper that, if he signed it, would save his life. Steadfastly he refused. At 4 p.m. he was led to the scaffold and beheaded.

Nobody wanted Franz to die. At least three priests and a bishop told him that it was not a sin to serve in the Nazi army; the bishop even urged that it was his duty to do so. The military tribunal that tried him also did its best to change his mind. But Franz remained unshakeable in his conviction. To serve the Nazi cause in any way was to betray God and his Catholic faith.

Franz Jägerstätter was not the only Catholic to be martyred at the hands of the Nazis. Several priests chose the same path. Franz's story is especially remarkable because he was a simple peasant with little formal education, yet his courage was based upon a profound spiritual understanding and total abandonment to the will of God.

His early life gave little promise of what was to come. He was born on May 24, 1907, in the tiny village of Saint Radegund in Upper Austria, close to the German border; the illegitimate son of a villager killed while fighting in World War I. In 1917 his mother married a local farmer and took the Jägerstätter name for herself and her son. At fourteen, Franz left school and went to work on the farm.

A powerfully-built teenager, he chased the girls and hung out with a gang that frequently battled with youths from neighboring villages — violent clashes in which the weapons included sand-filled thongs edged with knife-blades. Later he left Saint Radegund for a job in the iron mines. His two-year absence may not have been entirely voluntary. An illegitimate child born in the village was widely thought to be his.

After his return, in 1936, he married a local girl, and the couple went to Rome on honeymoon. Soon they had three daughters.

During his teenage years the brawling, girl-chasing Franz had continued to attend Mass and to observe the outward forms of religion; in a rural, deeply Catholic community, the social pressure to do so would have been strong. He himself described his religious practice at this time as "half-baked."

Many erring young men are altered for the better by marriage and fatherhood, but Franz underwent a change far beyond the normal. Now his faith was at the center of his life, and he began to show a spiritual maturity far beyond his years.

Undoubtedly his wife's influence played its part; she was a devout Catholic, and he loved her dearly. The honeymoon trip to Rome also may have had an impact. The pastor at Saint Radegund was a strong-minded, independent man, with whom Franz had many discussions when he became sacristan at the church. He also spoke much with a cousin who had joined a fundamentalist Protestant sect. Its members refused military service and paid the price. While rejecting their beliefs, Franz admired their courage.

How radical was his conversion we may judge from a letter he wrote to his fatherless young godson, Franz Huber, who was about to enter upon his own adolescence. It would have been written around 1936, the year of Franz Jägerstätter's marriage.

He warns young Huber against people who take the sixth commandment lightly, and calls those who laugh at it "devils in human form." Urging Huber to fix his eyes on the eternal homeland, he adds: "Though we must bear our sorrows and reap little reward in this world for doing so, we can still become richer than millionaires — for those who need not fear death are the richest and happiest of all."

He advises the youngster, when troubled by religious doubt, to reflect on the miracles and the saints that the Catholic faith has produced.

"Since the death of Christ, almost every century has seen the persecution of Christians; there have always been heroes and martyrs who gave their lives — often in horrible ways — for Christ and their faith," he says. "If we hope to reach our own goal someday, then we, too, must become heroes of the faith."

As Nazi aggression grew, so did Franz Jägerstätter's conviction that he could not be loyal both to Christ and to Hitler. In a vivid dream, he saw the Nazi party as a train, carrying its passengers to hell. He firmly believed that the dream was a message from God, an answer to the question: "Should I be a Nazi — or a Catholic?" In 1938 he voted against the *Anschluss*, the German takeover of Austria. He was the only man in the village to do so.

Because he was a farmer, his draft was twice deferred, but on February 25, 1943, he was ordered to report to the recruiting center. As he left the village, a neighbor called: "God go with you, Franz!" Quietly, Franz replied: "You will see no more of me."

Before responding to the draft order, Franz had spent an hour with Bishop Fliesser of Linz, who tried to convince him that his first responsibility was to his wife and children. Like many other Church leaders, the bishop took the view that the state must be obeyed in temporal matters, and that it was not for the individual citizen to make moral judgments about the war.

His arguments did nothing to shake Franz's conviction. At the draft center, he refused to register for military service and was arrested. During the months he spent in prison, in Linz and later in Berlin, chaplains urged him, as Bishop Fliesser had done, to put his wife and family first. Franz gently pushed their arguments aside.

Not even his wife's pleas could deflect him from his course, even though their eldest daughter was only six. He told her that he must obey God, not Hitler.

His jailers treated him humanely, impressed by his courage and serenity. Walking the prison corridors, he said the Rosary openly. He shared his bread ration with fellow prisoners and showed what other acts of kindness he could. On one occasion, he asked his wife to send some edelweiss for a condemned Frenchman, so that the little mountain flowers could be sent with a last letter to a girlfriend in France.

Before the military tribunal began its hearing, Franz's lawyer made a further attempt to save his life. In a highly unusual move, he begged the tribunal members first to interview his client informally and to try to persuade him to change his mind. Remarkably, they agreed.

The officers told Franz what he already knew, that if he persisted in his refusal they would have no alternative but to sentence him to death. Franz assured them that he fully understood his position, and that he could not in conscience fight for a regime that was persecuting his Church. Echoing Bishop Fliesser's arguments, the officers drew a distinction between support for the Nazi regime and the defense of the Fatherland. An ordinary citizen, they insisted, could not make a competent judgment on such a complicated issue.

When they saw that Franz remained unmoved, the officers virtually pleaded with him not to force them to condemn him. They guaranteed that if he signed up for military service he would not be required to fight, but would be given some form of noncombatant duty. Franz rejected the proposed compromise as immoral: He could not undertake any role that gave support to the regime. To do so, he told them, would be to commit an added sin of falsehood, by seeming to accept military service in order to escape the guillotine.

Realizing that they could not save him, the tribunal members went into formal session. The hearing was brief: Franz Jägerstätter was sentenced to death.

During his last days a prison chaplain, Father Jochmann, asked Franz to write a formal declaration of his point of view. For a man of his limited education it is a remarkable document, carefully argued and lucidly expressed.

Despite his own courageous stand, he refuses to condemn the bishops and priests who chose to compromise with the Nazi rulers after the *Anschluss*.

"They, too, are men like us, made of flesh and blood, and can weaken," he writes. "They are probably much more sorely tempted by the evil enemy than the rest of us. ... Perhaps, too, our bishops thought it would be only a short time before everything would come apart at the seams again and that, by their compliance, they would spare the faithful many agonies and martyrs. Unfortunately, things turned out to be quite different: Years have passed and thousands of people must now die in the grip of error every year."

The situation of Christians living under Nazi rule is, he declares, worse than that of early Christians in the time of their bloodiest persecutions.

"Many will perhaps ask themselves why God had to make us live in such a time as this. But we may not accuse God on this account, nor should we put the blame on others. There is an old saying: 'He who makes his bed must lie on it.' And it is still possible for us, even today, with God's help, to lift ourselves out of the mire in which we are stuck and win eternal happiness — if only we make a sincere effort and bring all our strength to the task."

Shortly before the execution, Father Jochmann entered Franz's cell and, in a final attempt to save him, pointed out the document lying on the table. Franz had only to sign it and his life would be spared. With a smile, Franz pushed it aside, repeating once again that he could not take an oath in favor of an unjust war.

The chaplain offered to bring some devotional booklets, or to read to him from the New Testament. Franz gently declined.

"I am completely bound in inner union with the Lord, and any reading would only interrupt my communion with my God," he said. As he spoke, Franz's eyes shone with such joy and confidence that the priest remembered his gaze to the end of his life.

Later the chaplain told some Austrian nuns: "I can only congratulate you on this countryman of yours who lived as a saint and has now died a hero. I say with certainty that this simple man is the only saint I ever met in my lifetime."

Before he died, Franz wrote: "Just as the man who thinks only of this world does everything possible to make life easier and better, so must we, too, who believe in the eternal kingdom, risk everything in order to receive a great reward there. Just as those who believe in National Socialism tell themselves that their struggle is for survival, so must we, too, convince ourselves that our struggle is for the eternal kingdom. But with this difference: We need no rifles or pistols for our battle, but instead, spiritual weapons — and the foremost among these is prayer. ... Through prayer, we continually implore new grace from God, since without God's help and grace it would be impossible for us to preserve the Faith and be true to His commandments ... .

"Let us love our enemies, bless those who curse us, pray for those who persecute us. For love will conquer and will endure for all eternity. And happy are those who live and die in God's love."

2

"COME SWEET DEATH
ON WEDNESDAY"

John Bradburne

On the night of September 2, 1979, ten teenage guerillas of the Patriotic Front descended on the Mutemwa Leprosy Camp at Mutoko, Rhodesia, and took away the warden, John Bradburne, a fifty-eight-year-old Englishman.

Knowing that John was deeply religious, they offered him girls to sleep with and subjected him to other taunts. Interrogated by the guerilla leaders, he knelt and prayed. The guerillas tried to persuade him to go with them to Mozambique to look after their people there.

John replied that his place was with the lepers at Mutemwa. He was totally unafraid.

In the evening of that day there was a Marxist consciousness-raising session for five hundred local people. A mother of twin babies asked him to look after them while she joined in, and they slept quietly in his lap.

During the early hours of the next morning, about fifty guerillas took John toward the main road. Before they reached it, the commander asked John to walk forward, then stop and face them. John did so. Again he knelt and prayed, still showing no sign of fear. The guerillas watched quietly.

After three minutes, he rose to his feet. As he did so, the guerilla commander shot him.

Why he was murdered will probably never be fully explained. It appears that the leaders were angry with the young cadets — known as *mujibhas* — for bringing him in, for he was widely known as a good, even saintly, man. Once he was in their hands, they seemed uncertain what to do with him. They may have decided, in the end, that he had seen too much to be allowed to live.

Although Rhodesia would soon gain its independence and become Zimbabwe, in 1979 the country was still torn by violence. By August there were only two white men left in the area of Mutoko, a trading post about seventy miles from the capital, Salisbury (now Harare). One was John Bradburne, the other a missionary, Father David Gibbs. It was Father Gibbs who found John's body beside the main road on the day after his death.

John Randal Bradburne was born in 1921 at Skirwith, Cumbria, in the northwest corner of England, an area of rolling hills and windswept moorland. As a boy, John roamed the countryside and learned to love birds, animals and all wild things — a love that would remain with him to the end of his life.

John's father was an Anglican minister, and the family was a cultured one. A cousin was the well-known playwright Terence Rattigan. While still a boy, John began to write poems, another lifelong passion.

No sooner had he left school in Norfolk than World War II began. Joining the Ghurkas, an Indian regiment, John was commissioned as an officer and was soon in Malaya. In 1942 the Japanese invaded and Singapore fell. John and his men were ordered to pair off and to avoid capture. For a month he lived in the jungle, with only roots, fruit, and a little rice for food.

An attempt to sail to Sumatra in a captured sampan ended in shipwreck. John and his companion, a brother officer, were washed ashore. Some days later they made a second attempt with a group of Scots soldiers. This time they were successful. The last British destroyer to leave Sumatra took John to safety.

Before long he was once more in the thick of the war, this time in Burma, where he fought with the Chindits. This specially trained force of jungle fighters flew far behind enemy lines to harry the Japanese occupying army and disrupt its communications. Before John and his men went into action, General Orde Wingate, the Chindits' legendary commander, singled out John on parade to congratulate him on his escape and on the Military Cross he had been awarded for bravery.

Brave John certainly was, yet his comrades noticed that he was reluctant to kill his fellow man. One recalled that in the depths of the jungle he spent much of his time birdwatching, singing psalms, and tending the wounded.

Before his escape from Malaya, the minister's son had shown no marked inclination toward the spiritual — for that we have the testimony of his brother, Philip. Apparently it was his war experiences, and perhaps also his encounter with Eastern religion, that set him on his quest for God.

During his army service in the Far East, John made a friend who was to play an important role in his life: John Dove, a fellow officer, later to become a Jesuit priest and John's biographer.

It was inevitable that John's spiritual search would lead him toward the Catholic Church, which attracted him strongly. The monastic ideal, especially, made a deep impression. When the war ended, he found his way to Buckfast Abbey, which was near his father's retirement home in Devon. There the Benedictine community welcomed him and gave him work in the monastery garden and cemetery. In 1947, on the feast of Christ the King, John was received into the Catholic Church.

He soon realized that the Benedictine life, which he greatly admired, was not for him. Instead John felt drawn to the Carthusians, whose regime of solitary work and prayer seemed more likely to meet his inner longings. At Parkminster, Sussex, Britain's only Charterhouse, he was given the job of doorkeeper;

but within months, his restless spirit was telling him to move on yet again.

Parkminster's prior advised John to go to Rome and ask Saint Peter to guide him to his true vocation. Once in Rome, John prayed and was convinced that Saint Peter gave him an answer: Go to Jerusalem. Arriving penniless in Haifa, he set out to walk to the capital. Then, as now, the political atmosphere in the Holy Land was tense. On the road John was arrested by Jewish forces who thought he might be a British spy, but he was quickly released.

Arriving safely in Jerusalem, he asked the way to the Mount Sion Benedictine monastery but was directed instead to the Fathers of Sion, a small order dedicated to the conversion of the Jews. John took the mistake as a sign from God and asked to join. The fathers sent him to their novitiate at Louvain, Belgium, but after a year the novice master realized that John was still in the wrong slot. He advised him to go back to Rome and pray again.

So John set off on foot to beg his way from Louvain to Rome. Once more he believed that Saint Peter was telling him to go to Jerusalem, but this time he had no means of getting there. Instead he walked south to the Appenine foothills, where a kindly village priest took him in and gave him a room in his church's organ loft. Here John wrote poems and prayed, playing the organ at night. Here, too, he vowed himself to Our Lady by a life of poverty and chastity.

A year after John's arrival, his father died, and he returned to England. For a time he tried to live as a hermit on the edge of Dartmoor, a large and rugged stretch of open country in southwest England. Without food or money, John soon found this impossible. Another spell with the Benedictines, this time at Prinknash, Gloucestershire, also did not last long. So he set off for London, playing madrigals on his recorder as he walked.

At Westminster Cathedral John was entranced by the music and joined the staff as a sacristan, hoping it would lead to a place in the choir. Instead, Cardinal William Godfrey appointed John caretaker of his country home in Hertfordshire. The work gave him time to pray and write poems, and he loved the peaceful atmosphere of the beautiful sixteenth-century house.

Along with the Scriptures, John read and reread *The Cloud of Unknowing*, the fourteenth-century spiritual classic by an unknown English writer that teaches the obliteration of self as a necessary preparation for mystical experience. The "cloud" of the title is the gulf between man and God, which can only be crossed by love and not by reason.

John had also become strongly drawn to the ideals of Saint Francis of Assisi. As we have seen, he always shared the gentle saint's love of birds and animals, and he was now a Franciscan tertiary.

When renovation began at the cardinal's country retreat, an army of workmen descended, and John's peace was shattered. He wrote to his army friend John Dove, now a Jesuit missionary in Rhodesia, to ask if there was a cave in Africa where he could pray.

With Father Dove's assistance, he found work as a helper at two Franciscan missions. But John's solitary nature made it difficult for him to fit in with the communities there. It was during this time that he confided his three wishes to a Franciscan priest: to serve leprosy patients, to die a martyr, and to be buried in the habit of Saint Francis. In time, all three were to be fulfilled.

In 1963, Lord and Lady Acton gave their home at Mbebi to the Society of Jesus. The Jesuits invited John to move in as caretaker. Once again, he was in his element, living a solitary life with two owls in the church roof for company.

In December of the following year, the Jesuit novices moved into the house at Mbebi, and John was invited to help

Father Dove open a center for leadership and development in their former home, Silveira House. Here, as before, he was a highly efficient caretaker who prayed and sang when not about his work. Father Dove believes that the success of the new center owed much to John's constant prayer.

The surrounding area was rich in woodland and wildlife, and John found a companion in the mission cat, which used to accompany him on his walks. He prayed for an eagle — and sure enough, an eagle made its home at the mission. But the center's success inevitably meant people and noise, so John moved first to the henhouse and then to a small room at the end of the building. His problem here was to ward off unwanted callers without seeming unkind, and he hit on a novel solution. A swarm of bees would, he decided, prove an ideal deterrent. So once again he prayed — and very soon, a swarm settled in his room.

By 1968 he was again restless, feeling that his work at Silveira House was done. John thought of seeking a hermit's cave in Israel or India. After a visit to his mother in England and a pilgrimage to the Holy Land, he knew that his vocation lay in Africa. So he returned to Zimbabwe.

In 1969 God granted John the first of his three wishes. Mutemwa Leprosy Camp was home to ninety patients who were living in squalid conditions with little care and in a state of spiritual desolation.

The lepers were dirty and hungry, their sores festering, the roofs of their huts falling in. Visiting the camp with a female friend, Heather Benoy, John declared: "I'm staying." He meant it quite literally. Heather, who had suggested the visit, was alarmed and pleaded with him to return to the capital with her. They argued for hours until at last, with Heather in tears, he agreed to go back and collect a few belongings. The Jesuits, who had been asked to help, invited John to become the camp's warden.

Though distressed by the misery that faced him at Mutemwa, John quickly realized that at last he had found his home. Because he himself felt an outcast from society — "I'm a drone," he used to say — John believed he had much in common with the lepers, who accepted him joyfully. John was grateful for their welcome, though he knew that he had few qualifications for the task ahead, and certainly no medical training. "It's bad enough to suffer from leprosy without having me as well," he said wryly.

Medical help soon arrived in the form of Dr. Luisa Guidotti, Sister Caterina, and Elizabeth Tarira, herself later to qualify as a doctor. The four transformed the camp into a place of tender loving care. John himself bathed and fed the patients, drove off the rats that often gnawed at their unfeeling limbs, and cut the nails of those who had fingers and toes. Each patient was his friend, and about each of them he wrote a poem. When they lay dying, he read the Gospel to them.

Meanwhile, he had a friend design a chapel, a small, round building equipped with a harmonium. Here John played Bach, taught the patients to sing Gregorian plainchant and — by special permission — distributed Holy Communion daily.

Despite the Jesuits' involvement, Mutemwa was under the secular control of the Rhodesia Leprosy Association. After Jesuit Father Edward Ennis retired from the camp management committee, John found himself at loggerheads with officials who considered him extravagant. Patients were allowed five dollars per month for food and other necessities; John was criticized for trying to provide a weekly loaf of bread for each patient. Dr. Guidotti, too, was accused of overspending on drugs and "unnecessary" travel.

Matters came to a head after John refused to put numbers around the patients' necks. "They are people, not cattle," he told his bosses. They fired him.

But it would take more than a bureaucratic ax to separate John from his beloved lepers. On Chigona, the mountain that overlooked the camp, he pitched a tent that became his home. The patients begged him to come down — there was a leopard out there on the great rock. John stayed, living the hermit's life he had craved for so long.

Dressed in his Franciscan habit, John prayed, wrote poems, and ministered to the lepers as best he could, often stealing into the camp by night. He grew his hair and beard long and ate hardly anything. "I have always wanted to fly, and I reckon that if I'm very thin I'll have more chance of doing it," he joked.

To give him better shelter and easier access to the camp, a kindly white farmer built John a tin hut outside the compound. Pauline Hutchings, wife of another farmer, brought him what little food he ate. Luisa Guidotti tried to tempt him with delicacies and brought him drugs for the lepers. Father David Gibbs, the only remaining missionary in the area, came each week to say Mass for John and the patients.

These friends showed great courage, for soon the war was all around them, and Father Gibbs could no longer reach his outlying Mass centers. Suddenly John fell ill — perhaps not surprisingly, given his severe lifestyle. Luisa managed to get him to a hospital in the capital, where he nearly died from a polio-type virus. Recovered, he convalesced at Silveira House before returning to Mutemwa.

All around him, the danger was growing; exploding landmines and gunfire were familiar sounds. An old man who came to Mass at Mutemwa was shot by young guerillas, apparently because he had once served with the British forces. John denounced the killers furiously, without regard for his own safety. Luisa, alarmed, begged him to curb his anger.

But nothing could prevent John from speaking out against evil, especially if his lepers were the victims. Herd boys who allowed cattle to eat the patients' maize, camp orderlies who cut down trees that shaded them, thieves who stole their rations ... all these felt the lash of his tongue. He was particularly hard on the African warden who had officially replaced him. It is scarcely surprising that he made enemies.

Before his own martyrdom, John had to suffer another cruel blow. Luisa was killed — gunned down in her ambulance as she drove to her patients in the surrounding countryside.

At the end of August, John told Coletta, the leper sacristan, that there was an evil spirit in his hut. She went to the hut and found a particular species of red ant, which for Shona people is an ill omen. John, uneasy, slept in the chapel for two nights.

The next night he spent on the mountain, Chigona, and came down quite changed. He told Coletta that he had seen "a big angel" there, and that all was well.

On Sunday, September 2, he gave Holy Communion to the lepers and preached to them about Saint Lawrence, the young deacon martyred by the Romans in the third century. He asked them to pray that he would face death with the same courage that Lawrence had shown.

Nobody saw the young *mujibhas* come for John. Voices were heard, and then silence. In one of his poems, he had written: "Come sweet death on Wednesday if you will and if you may." It was close to dawn on Wednesday, September 5, when the guerilla leader shot him.

At his funeral in the capital, a friend placed three white flowers on the coffin, to symbolize his devotion to the Trinity. Soon afterward, Jesuit Father Michael O'Halloran was amazed to see a drop of fresh red blood fall from the coffin onto the floor of the sanctuary. When Father O'Halloran placed a cloth over it, two more drops fell.

After the funeral the coffin was opened and the body inspected. There was no sign of anything that could account for the blood. However, it was noticed that John was wearing a shirt. After his death, Father Gibbs had removed John's Franciscan habit from his hut, but had forgotten to see that he was dressed in it. Now the habit was brought, and John's third request fulfilled.

Three wishes, three flowers, three drops of blood ... in view of these apparent signs, and of John's evident holiness, it is scarcely surprising that many believe him a saint. Some who knew him tell stories of being visited by eagles and swarms of bees. A guardian of his shrine at Mutemwa claims to have seen Our Lady appear there. Miracles have been claimed, including the cure of a woman suffering from terminal cancer.

A file of material for John's beatification was submitted in 1986, but the archbishop of Harare ruled that it was too early to proceed and that it would be prudent to await further evidence. If John is beatified, it may not be for many years.

Meanwhile, his life of prayer, his devotion to Christ in his suffering lepers, his absolute refusal to compromise with the world, his total disregard for money and power — all these surely make John Bradburne a prophet for our materialistic age:

> *Now let me tell you this,*
> *you pilgrims all*
> *Love is a long desire*
> *a short disease,*
> *An everlasting healing*
> *and a call. ...*

3

"I SAW JESUS MOVING THROUGH THE WORLD"

Venerable Marthe Robin

During the fifty years from 1931 to 1981, some one hundred thousand people traveled to a farmhouse near Lyons, France, to visit an invalid who lay totally paralyzed in a darkened room.

Rich and poor, priests and layfolk, intellectuals and simple peasants — all brought their troubles, hopes, or fears to Marthe Robin, herself a farmer's daughter with little formal education. Each stayed for ten minutes, during which time Marthe would listen, advise, and then invite her guest to say a prayer with her.

Nobody left Marthe's presence without being profoundly affected. Sometimes the interview changed the visitor's life.

At thirty-three, Yves de Boisredon, a prosperous wine merchant, had no thought of a career change when he sat down beside Marthe's divan. In a life crammed with worldly pleasures, Yves had become indifferent about his faith. Ten minutes later he left convinced that he was called to the priesthood. He duly entered the seminary and was ordained.

One of the twentieth century's greatest mystics, Marthe Robin bore the stigmata and each Friday experienced all the pains of Christ's Passion and Crucifixion. She never slept. Unable to ingest food or to drink even water, she was sustained solely by the Eucharist, which she received each week.

Yet from her sickbed she organized aid for prisoners and the poor, established two schools, produced a wealth of spiritual writing, and founded the Foyers of Charity, a movement that has spread across the world.

Marthe was born on March 13, 1902, at Chateauneuf-de-Galaure, in southeastern France, the youngest of six children. The next year, her five-year-old sister, Clemence, died in a typhoid epidemic.

Marthe survived, but from then on her health was fragile. Despite this she was a bright, happy child who loved to sing, dance, and play games.

Her first Holy Communion at the age of ten affected her profoundly. She always believed that at that moment, our Lord called her to live only for him.

Deeply devoted to Our Lady, she recited the Rosary at every opportunity; while walking into the village and in bed at night.

She attended the village school until she was thirteen. Then, like other children of that time, she left to work on the family farm.

In November 1918, Marthe was struck down by encephalitis. For twenty-seven months she lay in a near coma and was given last rites.

Soon afterward she recovered sufficiently to sit in the farmhouse kitchen, where she occupied herself with knitting and embroidery. However, paralysis was slowly spreading through her body.

Marthe was nineteen when Our Lady first appeared to her. Over the years she was to see not only the Blessed Virgin, but also our Lord and Saint Thérèse of Lisieux, to whom she had a particular devotion.

In October 1926 she became so ill that she was again given last rites. In a vision, Saint Thérèse told Marthe that she had a choice: to go to heaven at once or to unite her sufferings with those of Christ in atonement for the sins of mankind, for the renewal of the Church, and for a Christian revival in France. Marthe's decision was instant.

Swiftly the devil tormented her with doubt, trying to persuade her that her suffering was useless. Later, unable to destroy her spiritually, he launched fierce physical attacks that continued to the day of her death.

Of her mission she declared: "I saw Jesus moving through the world, laden with his cross, searching for souls to bear it with him; but they all ran away at his approach . . . so once more I offered myself."

The value of suffering, willingly accepted, is a constant theme in her writings, which she dictated to friends. "Sickness is a wonderful grace, an incomparable richness," she said.

On October 3, 1930, the feast day of Saint Thérèse, Jesus appeared to her crucified. Tongues of fire from his wounds pierced her, and he pressed the crown of thorns upon her head. The wounds appeared upon her body, and from then on she relived the Passion each Friday, remaining as if dead until the following Sunday.

After her weekly Communion, Marthe went into ecstasy. Witnesses testified that they saw the Host fly from the priest's hand into her mouth.

Our Lord told her that he would entrust her with a great project, and that he would send a priest to help her. In February 1936, Father Georges Finet, a priest of the Lyons archdiocese, became her spiritual director.

Seven months later, the first Foyer of Charity was established in Marthe's home village, and Father Finet preached the first retreat. Today there are seventy-five foyers in thirty-two countries.

A Foyer of Charity is a dedicated community of lay people working under the direction of a priest, the Father of the Foyer, and welcoming those who come on retreat.

In French, *foyer* means both "hearth and "home." Our Lord told Marthe that a Foyer must be a place "radiant with light, charity, and love." Retreats last for five or six days, as Marthe declared that three days were "not enough to change a soul."

The retreats are held in complete silence, apart from the prayers and the preaching of the Father of the Foyer. They are designed to lead to a complete renewal in the faith of those taking part.

In 1940 Marthe became blind, having offered her sight to God for the salvation of France. Despite her suffering she remained cheerful and practical, with a countrywoman's robust sense of humor. She loved children, and did not like her adult visitors to take themselves too seriously.

When a well-known philosopher, Marcel Clement, entered her room, Marthe startled him by chatting about her goat, which he had passed as he entered the farmhouse.

Thirty years later, when they had become firm friends, the philosopher asked:

"Marthe, do you remember our first meeting? You talked to me about your goat."

"Yes," Marthe replied. "You needed to be brought down to earth."

She took a lively interest in the world outside and was delighted by the election of Pope John Paul II. "Our Lady has done us a good turn there!" she declared.

Marthe died on February 6, 1981, a month before her seventy-ninth birthday. The cause for her beatification, opened in 1991, is already well-advanced.

4

"AVOID EVERYTHING HALF-DONE"

Venerable Edel Quinn

One summer day in 1927, a young Frenchman leaned across the table of a Dublin restaurant and gazed into the eyes of the beautiful Irish girl opposite.

"Edel, I love you," he said quietly. "Will you marry me?"

A girl often knows when a proposal is coming — but not this time. Completely taken aback, Edel flushed and looked down, hating the pain she was about to inflict. Then, bracing herself, she gave her answer.

"I can't marry you, Pierre," she told her suitor gently. "You see, I'm already promised, to God. I'm going to become a Poor Clare nun."

A few months before, Pierre, an importer of building materials, had taken her on as secretary at his office in Tara Street. Now he was moving to London, and he had hoped to take Edel with him as his wife.

Pierre took his rejection badly, sobbing his way across the Irish Sea until the boat reached Liverpool. Edel, meanwhile, was worried not only because she had disappointed him but because she feared he might lapse in his practice of the Catholic faith, to which he had returned under her influence.

For many years, Edel wrote him regularly. Each birthday she sent him a present — which sometimes caused problems.

"I am glad you liked the tie," said one relieved missive. "I was on pins and needles trying to choose it, because nobody can choose a tie for a man except that man himself! It was the red stripes that gave me spasms. I was afraid they might displease your majesty's taste ... I spent from one until two choosing it, and the girl was nearly frantic at the end."

A beatification process is a serious business, but those who examine Edel's writings find many such lines as those to lighten their task. She never became a Poor Clare, but many are confident that one day she will be declared a saint.

Edel Mary Quinn was born in Greenane, a tiny village in County Cork, on September 14, 1907. Her unusual first name was a mistake; her mother had intended to call her Adele. However, the priest wrote "Edel" in the baptismal register, and Edel she remained.

An excellent photograph exists of Edel at four. Even then she was a real Irish beauty, her sweet open face with its wide-set eyes and firm chin framed by long tresses. The smile shows serenity and intelligence astonishing in a child of her age.

At school her teachers soon realized that here indeed was an exceptional young lady — though they would have hesitated to call her a saint! "She was a real imp," recalled one, "never cheeky, but always bubbling over with good spirits, full of life and gaiety and up to every kind of prank. She was the center of every group bent on fun or mischief."

Cycling at full speed down the hill that led from the convent to the town, Edel would often turn and wave to show that she was in full control. She loved tennis, dancing, and playing the piano.

The camera had not lied: At ten she had a poise that many a grown woman might have envied. Instinctively, she did and said the right thing. Not even a visiting bishop overawed her; she chatted away with a perfect mixture of freedom and deference.

But poise is one thing, holiness another. It was her family who first recognized Edel's real worth. "Never did we see a trace of selfishness in her," they said later. "She forgot herself completely for the sake of others, and she did it as a matter of course."

She was more than bright enough for college, but her family's needs forced her, at nineteen, to take the job with Pierre. While her sights were set firmly on the Poor Clares, she knew that she would have to work for several years before she could think of entering the convent.

Although Edel had made a practicing Catholic of him, Pierre never suspected her ambition until his proposal of marriage forced her to break the news. At work she was as keen and capable as any career girl — so much so that after Pierre left for England, Edel herself became manager in his stead.

She was still a talented dancer and had taken up a new sport — golf. She spent much of her time at a social club, playing the piano and running amateur theatricals.

Yet this fun-loving miss usually heard seven Masses each Sunday morning and was back in church for Benediction in the afternoon. To do some act of kindness she would readily go without lunch, and her mortification did not end there. Soon her life was one long Lent. Whenever possible she took her tea without milk or sugar, and her bread without butter. Breakfast was often an apple, tucked into her purse and eaten on the train that took her to work. Even on the coldest nights she would not entertain a hot-water bottle.

Nevertheless she never thought well of herself, never regarded herself as somebody special. "I have asked Our Lady to look after you and to do what is best for you," she wrote Pierre, "so you are in good hands. Please do not say that you are not worthy, Pierre; it is not true; you are far above me in every way. God knows that, and it is only his merciful love that could call me to serve him in religion, seeing what I am . . ." Small wonder that Pierre, who eventually married a Frenchwoman, named one of his daughters for Edel.

Her regime of prayer and penance was, of course, a preparation for her entry into the Poor Clares. But soon she had a new motivation, one that was to take over her whole life. For during these years of waiting, Edel joined the Legion of Mary.

"I'm not sure that she is very suitable," said the friend who introduced her. "She is a very vivacious, lighthearted girl. She might find our work too hard and monotonous."

Mona Tierney, who had not known Edel for long, was not the first to underestimate her, nor was she the last. Anyone deceived by Edel's gaiety ought to have taken a good look into her eyes — remarkably beautiful eyes, certainly, but piercing and full of determination. For a picture taken when she was twenty-eight, Edel obviously took great care to look as attractive as possible. Makeup, necklace, hairstyle, pretty dress — all these set off her beauty to the full. But it is the eyes that rivet the attention. Their force strikes out even from the printed page.

In the Legion, Edel found that force harnessed: At the end of her first meeting she was totally committed. Soon she was devoting every spare moment to the work, visiting sick and lonely people, praying with and for them, winning them with her gaiety and charm. With one paranoid old woman Edel would sit for hours at a time, until she finally persuaded her that the neighbors were not really out to get her.

The Legion had been founded in Dublin only a few years earlier by a civil servant named Frank Duff. Organized along Roman military lines, dedicated to Our Lady as Mediatrix of All Graces, it set out to provide spiritual help however and whenever needed. Its earliest and most spectacular successes were among the prostitutes who teemed in some of the city's most squalid tenements. The first members braved threats and insults, not only from the girls but also from their pimps, in order to get them back to God.

After a two-year apprenticeship in the ranks, Edel was herself transferred to this work as president of a praesidium — the small group that is the Legion's basic unit. Her arrival sent a deputation of members to headquarters to inquire politely whether headquarters had gone off its head.

How, demanded the protesters, could a slip of a girl in her early twenties lead them in their mission among Dublin's most degraded citizens? Surely they ought to have as their president a mature woman, someone tough and experienced — not this frail Miss Quinn.

"We know her, you don't. She's your new president, and that's it. So, back to work!"

I do not imagine that headquarters put it quite so bluntly as that. But the message was clear enough. The protesters departed, no doubt expecting disaster. They soon found out what Edel was made of.

When two members, because of a misunderstanding about their rendezvous, failed to carry out their Sunday-morning assignment, Edel said little. Later, in private, she delivered a rebuke that one offender, at least, never forgot.

"An appointment to do Legion work is an appointment with Our Lady," she declared. "If you had visited that lodging house, as you were asked, you might have got a woman out to Mass. And that would have meant one mortal sin less."

She spent much of her time at Sancta Maria, the hostel the Legion ran for the women it had rescued. She was a great favorite with the girls there, using all her talent for dancing and theatricals to keep them amused.

Yet she drove herself hard — so hard that her friends began to worry.

"If you are not careful we'll soon be having a requiem for another dead legionary," a friend warned her as they attended a funeral.

"That would be fine!" was Edel's laughing retort.

Absorbed though she was in Legion work, she never for a moment wavered in her determination to become a nun. By 1932 her family no longer depended on her wages. Excitedly, she arranged to enter the Poor Clares' convent in Belfast.

Suddenly, Edel suffered a hemorrhage of the lungs. A doctor told her the worst. She had advanced tuberculosis.

The diagnosis ended her hopes, as she must have realized even then. Yet she bore it with all her usual cheerfulness. "Circumstances are the sacraments of God's will" — Edel wrote that, and she believed it. She went, not to the convent but to a sanatorium in County Wicklow, where she spent the next eighteen months.

"She made everyone around her happy . . . she would often laugh until the tears came," a friend recalled later. Her best friend at the sanatorium was a Protestant girl, and the matron, also a Protestant, grew to love Edel dearly.

Despite her illness, she continued to refuse hot-water bottles, and she did not have many sheets. Nothing could stop her passion for mortifying herself.

When she returned home, she was still far from well. Her health did not improve in the months that followed, though she obeyed the doctors faithfully. She took a secretarial job in a Dublin garage, in an office so dark that the electric light was switched on all the time. More unpleasant still were the fumes that drifted in constantly through the open door. For a TB sufferer, these conditions were just about the worst imaginable.

Once again she flung herself into Legion work. Early in 1936, ignoring the usual protests from her friends, she used her two-week vacation to take part in a Legion recruiting drive in North Wales. She returned, not exhausted as her friends had gloomily prophesied, but filled with a great new idea. Her recruiting drive would become permanent: To spread the work of the Legion, she would leave her beloved Ireland and settle in Chester, the ancient English city at the gateway to Wales.

Before she could make any preparations, a more dramatic call sent her blood racing. Edel was asked to go as Legion envoy to Africa.

If you think it crazy that anyone with Edel's medical history should even be considered for such a mission, you are in good company. At least one member of the Concilium, the Legion's governing body, shared that view. The formidable Dr. Magennis, ex-General of the Calced Carmelites, roared his disapproval. He had spent years in Africa, and he knew the hardships Edel would meet there. He proceeded to set them out in frightening detail.

When he paused for breath, Edel spoke up quietly. "I know what I am going to and it is exactly what I want," she said. "I don't want to go on any picnic."

A picnic it certainly was not. On the evening of Saturday, October 24, 1936, Edel Quinn sailed from Dublin on the first leg of her journey to Kenya. She never saw Ireland again.

The story of her labors in Africa has been fully documented by Cardinal Suenens, who wrote Edel's official biography in 1952. In East Africa, in Mauritius, in South Africa, and finally back in Kenya, the frail Irish girl labored with the vigor of a Patrick or a Columba. Along roads whose dust choked her diseased lungs, through seas of mud that left her black from head to foot, she traveled endlessly. Sometimes she hitched lifts, sometimes she drove a battered old Ford that she called her "Rolls Royce." Always the object was the same: to set up the Legion where it did not exist, and to foster and encourage it where it did.

Once she arrived back unexpectedly at a convent where she was staying and found that the nuns had gone to bed. Rather than wake them, she stretched out on the veranda and spent a bitterly cold night there, covered only by her thin blue coat.

The nuns, upset, made her promise not to do such a thing again.

"If the same situation arose," Edel replied, "I'd have to do exactly the same." And soon afterward, that is exactly what happened. This time Edel was ill when the nuns found her. They had to put her to bed.

"They tell me here that I have vastly changed," she wrote Legion headquarters in Dublin. "Some who knew me well declare that never would they recognize me — except the voice, the rest was different. Also my hair is graying: Old age creeps on."

In fact Edel was still in her early thirties, but when she eventually went into a South African nursing home, the nuns thought she was sixty. At one time her weight dropped to seventy-five pounds.

"Avoid everything half-done," Edel once wrote in her private spiritual notes. If she had a motto, that was it. Although she recovered some of her strength, the improvement was only temporary, for she refused to let up. Inexorably, tuberculosis took hold once more. From Kenya she reported: "I can do a solid day's writing without overstrain, but the walking gets me! After a short distance I am finished."

Even when she could no longer walk, she went on writing. Sometimes she wrote as many as forty letters a day; cheerful letters to friends at home, and letters of advice and direction to fellow legionaries all over Africa.

"Pray for me and keep on joking, so that I shan't break down," she had begged a friend as she left Ireland for the last time. Edel's letters were full of jokes, yet what she suffered inwardly we can judge from an incident just before she left Mauritius. She had been particularly happy there, and as she made her round of farewell calls, she suddenly began to sob.

"Always my life is like this," she told her companion. "As soon as I have made real friends I have to break off and face the unknown." It was one of the few times that anyone saw Edel cry.

Her patience, also, must often have been tried. "Sometimes one would give much for a long evening at Regina Coeli just to let off a little steam," she wrote a friend ruefully. Yet to everyone she was kindly and serene. Never was she harsh or ill-tempered.

As a child she had prayed every day to be a martyr. In Africa she suffered a long, slow martyrdom, joyfully undertaken.

It ended at Nairobi, in the garden of a convent, in the evening of May 12, 1944. Earlier in the day, Edel had tried on a new dressing gown with real pleasure, and she spent a quiet afternoon sitting out in a deck chair. At 6:15 she suddenly collapsed.

She had known that she would die before long, but now that the moment had come, it seemed to take her by surprise. "Is Jesus coming?" she asked the mother superior, bewildered. When the priest arrived to anoint her, she smiled. By this time she could no longer speak. The nuns carried her to her room and placed the Legion statue of Our Lady beside her. There, soon afterward, the end came.

For her burial in the missionaries' cemetery, the Sisters of the Precious Blood, who had looked after her, dressed her in their own habit. Edel, who had wanted so much to become a nun, became one in death.

Her gravestone speaks warmly of her devotion and courage. It says, truly, that the Legion of Mary and Africa will be forever in her debt. Yet, years before, Edel had written an even better epitaph for herself:

"We have only this life, and perhaps a short one, in which to prove our love."

5

"DYING IS A FULL-TIME JOB"

Father Vincent McNabb, O.P.

*I*t is a Sunday early in 1943 in London's Hyde Park. From the Catholic Evidence Guild platform an elderly Dominican makes an announcement to his open-air audience:

"I am sorry, but I shall not be able to conduct the Stations of the Cross for you on Good Friday. You see, I am going to die soon."

The words are spoken quietly, almost casually. The audience, Catholics and hecklers alike, is stunned. Some of them quite simply refuse to believe what they have heard.

"Father McNabb, surely there's some mistake," says his favorite heckler. "You can't mean what you are saying."

"It's true," Father Vincent McNabb assures him calmly. "I am going to die, perhaps in a week, perhaps in a fortnight."

He has, he explains, got cancer of the throat, and the doctors can do nothing more. "In any case," he adds cheerfully. "I am an old man."

In fact, Father Vincent *did* conduct the Good Friday Stations. He did not die until the following June, three weeks before his seventy-fifth birthday. "I don't propose to take death lying down," he declared, and he did not. He spoke in Hyde Park, he carried out his parish duties, and he gave interviews to newspapers on the subject of his approaching end.

When he knew the time was near, he gave detailed instructions to a young colleague about his funeral. His coffin, of plain deal, was to be carried to the cemetery on the back of a builder's truck.

"I know what people will say. They'll say it's McNabb and his tomfoolery — it's just another of his stunts. But it isn't that. It's my last sermon," he declared.

Though he got the coffin of his choice, his superiors vetoed the truck. Vincent McNabb went to his grave in a conventional hearse. His dying remark shows how well he understood his critics.

"To me he was not a saint but a poseur . . . just a mass of eccentricities," wrote a fellow Dominican after his death. Another Dominican remarked to me dryly: "If Vincent gets canonized, there's hope for us all."

Yet seven years after Vincent died, Edward Siderman, the favorite heckler I mentioned earlier, published a book of recollections about him. Mr. Siderman, a Jew, called the book *A Saint in Hyde Park*.

"Ah," you may say. "Mr. Siderman knew him only on Sunday afternoons. His fellow Dominicans had to live with him." Indeed. But by no means would all have sided with the two I have just quoted. Some certainly thought Edward Siderman nearer the mark.

Saint, buffoon — or both? Today, surely, nobody can read even the briefest account of his life without doubting his very real holiness.

He was born the seventh of eleven children, at Portaferry, Northern Ireland, on July 7, 1868. His baptismal name was Joseph, and throughout his life he retained a strong devotion to his patron.

As the entire world knows, Northern Ireland is a tough place for a Catholic youngster to grow up, especially if he is poor. The McNabbs were very poor, yet, thanks to their strong faith, also very happy. "Holy Mass was the center of our day," Vincent recalled later. "The love of it was in our very blood."

His father was a stern sea captain, often away from home. His mother, Ann, was gentle but a woman of exceptional character. As a girl she emigrated to New York, worked as a dressmaker, and was soon in demand among rich wives. When her employer's son proposed marriage, however, she turned him down and went home to Ireland, afraid that a prosperous life in the United States might endanger her faith. Her son inherited her horror of wealth and kept it to the end of his days.

From the beginning, Joe was not strong. When two doctors told his mother that he would not survive a spinal complaint, she took him to a third, who cured him in two years. In later life, as we have seen, he was often regarded as an attention-seeker. Possibly he became so through growing up a sickly child among rambunctious older brothers.

Argumentative he certainly was. One evening his father, hearing the boys quarreling loudly, came to see what it was all about.

"Joe says he could become president of the United States," the others explained, "and we say he couldn't because he wasn't born there."

"Joe, you know your brothers are right, so why are you arguing?" Captain McNabb demanded.

"I could become the president," replied Joe smugly, "if God wished it."

But he was, too, a deeply affectionate child. To the end of his life he remembered the day when, at age six, he was suddenly hit in the face by a boy whom he thought his best pal. "Something seemed to go dead inside me," he recalled. "Perhaps it has never come to life again."

He thought of becoming a diocesan priest, but before he could enter a seminary, the family moved to England. In Newcastle-upon-Tyne, their new hometown, there was a large Dominican parish. Joe soon realized that his future lay with the Order of Preachers. At eighteen, Joe McNabb became Brother Vincent.

"I went into the religious life because it seemed the easiest way of avoiding eternal punishment," he wrote later. "As I didn't want to go to hell, I went to Woodchester."

They were golden days at the novitiate in the Gloucestershire countryside. One day his novice-master took him for a walk and explained religious obedience — evidently with some success. "Afterwards I thought to myself, 'That's good. Isn't it a marvelous thing, this idea of obedience?'" he said later.

Obedience did nothing to curb his boyish exuberance, nor did ordination. Villagers soon ceased being surprised at the mad young friar who rode a cycle without brakes down a frighteningly steep hill and finished up in a hedge, or who jousted in knightly fashion with one of his brethren, each with a small boy on his back.

Long before the Dominicans established their novitiate there, Woodchester had been visited by Blessed Dominic Barberi, the Italian priest who received John Henry Newman into the Church. He got a mocking reception and, according to legend, laid a curse on the village so that no Catholic family ever came to live there.

When Vincent heard the story, he decided that enough was enough: Woodchester had now expiated its rudeness to the saintly Passionist. Armed with holy water and flanked by acolytes, he marched through the streets sprinkling vigorously right and left. Sure enough, a Catholic leaven soon appeared in the Protestant lump.

But if Vincent was making a name for himself as an eccentric, he was also making one as a teacher and a preacher, for he had an incisive brain and a profound knowledge both of the Bible and of Saint Thomas Aquinas, whose works he helped to translate into English. He was awarded the degree of master of theology, the order's highest academic honor.

Vincent would certainly have been happy as a great Dominican scholar, working among the books and manuscripts he loved so much. But he loved people more, and it was among people that his vocation flourished.

In the earlier years of his priesthood, he served several communities, sometimes as prior. He was not an easy superior, partly because he demanded the best from everyone, himself included. At Leicester, where he was parish priest for a time, he chided the Saint Vincent de Paul Society when he learned that it had a small balance in hand. The money, he felt, should have gone to help the poor without delay. "I hope and pray that there will soon be a deficit," he said.

When a new church was planned at Leicester, Vincent sailed for the United States to raise money for the project. During the voyage, his fellow passengers elected him concert chairman. In his element, he regaled them with comic songs.

"Curiously enough, New York does not give me the idea of hustle," he wrote. "It has an almost opposite atmosphere of dignity and decorum."

His mission was not a success: A month's preaching netted only $450, and soon he was on his way home, concluding sadly, "the McNabbs were not meant to be beggars."

During his time at Leicester, a group of women tertiaries put themselves under his spiritual direction. In due course they adopted the Carmelite rule, established a community and emigrated to the United States, where they now have several houses.

In 1920 Vincent returned to the Dominicans' London parish at Haverstock Hill, where he had worked briefly some years before. Here he remained until his death and here, his admirers believe, he reached great heights of holiness.

He did not, of course, reach them easily. All his life Vincent McNabb fought a mighty battle with himself, and it was because he fought it publicly that he was so often called poseur, play-actor, and attention-seeker.

Perhaps his biggest temptation was to intellectual arrogance. The boy who quarreled with his brothers still could not bear to lose an argument. Once, when the London community was entertaining a distinguished Redemptorist, an argument blew up about the use of the term "Roman Catholic." The Redemptorist held that it was offensive, a Protestant jibe implying that the Church was an alien body. Vincent took the contrary view. The words "Roman" and "Catholic" were, he insisted, part of the Church's official title; therefore, the description was proper.

The argument grew heated, most of the Dominicans siding with the guest. Finally, flushed with anger, Vincent jumped up. "You're wrong — you're all wrong," he yelled, and stamped out of the room. The following day, overcome with remorse, he publicly asked forgiveness of his brethren and, as prescribed in the Rule, prostrated himself in penance before them.

Preaching in a fashionable London church, Vincent got on to the subject of Protestant errors. Somewhat carried away by his own rhetoric, he stopped suddenly and clapped a hand to his mouth. "Oh, my God — I have been uncharitable," he cried in horror. Begging pardon of his congregation, he knelt down facing the altar and asked God's forgiveness for his shortcomings toward the separated brethren.

On the other hand, he was merciless in denouncing evil. Invited to a eugenicists' meeting, he listened quietly to the speeches and then rose to make his own. "You have been advocating the sterilization of moral degenerates," he said. "Well, I am a moral expert and I certify *you* as moral degenerates. Good afternoon."

At Catholic Evidence Guild meetings he never lost his temper whatever the provocation, nor did he show anger or irritation toward even the rudest hecklers. One heckler did, however, upset his equilibrium: He called Vincent a liar. Vincent, deeply wounded, got down from the platform and walked away.

On the following Sunday, when he arrived at the pitch, the heckler was waiting. Vincent walked straight up to him, apologized for his anger of the previous week, then knelt down and kissed his feet. Ignoring alike the shouts of "play-actor" from his opponents and the embarrassment of his fellow speakers, Vincent mounted the platform and delivered his lecture in sparkling style.

Often, when the heckling was rough, Catholics in the crowd would get angry. As every CEG speaker knows, this is a particularly difficult situation to handle, one that can explode into violence if not controlled quickly. Vincent was adept at cooling tempers.

"Questioners are our guests," he would say, "and they have a right to disagree with us. Many of you will learn more about your religion from these questions and answers than you have done at school or at church."

As Vincent himself observed, it was not generally the devout who caused the trouble. Some Catholics only seem to remember their faith when they hear it attacked.

Once, when a lapsed Catholic was particularly offensive, Vincent begged his outraged co-religionists to pray for him — and for themselves, that they might not go the same way. "The faith is hard to gain but easy to lose," he said. "Even I could lose it, so pray for me, too!"

Some of the crowd must have smiled at that prospect, but although Vincent was sure of his faith, he was never sure of himself. When Cardinal Griffin of Westminster visited the friars, he asked jocularly: "Father Vincent, what would you do if the Reds descended on Haverstock Hill?"

"Your Eminence, I should apostatize at once," replied Vincent.

Everyone, including the cardinal, roared with laughter. Vincent did not laugh.

Yet nobody proclaimed his faith more joyfully or confidently. "I have a Catholic heart, a rationalist head, and a Protestant stomach," he would tell his audiences to their delight, and he insisted that it was his rationalist head that kept him in the Church.

His stomach indeed protested too much, and he also suffered badly from migraines; yet he insisted on carrying out his duties even when so ill that he could hardly stand. Despite his eccentricity, he had a horror of "singularity" — of being treated in any way differently from his brethren. He suffered agonies when his prior, noticing that kippers upset him, ordered that he be served boiled eggs instead.

Self-pity he could not stand, in himself or in others. A colleague, sleepless with worry, came to his room one night and announced: "I'm afraid I'm going to die."

"My dear brother," replied Vincent. "If you are to be worthy of our dear Lord, you must try to overcome these fears. Now, if you are really going to die, please go to your room and do it."

The priest did not die. As he later admitted, he began to feel better from that moment.

Yet this same Vincent McNabb showed the utmost patience with a senile colleague whom others found exceptionally trying. No matter how busy Vincent was, he never missed a nightly game of checkers with the old man, and somehow contrived always to let him win.

Nor was his charity confined to his brethren. A district nurse, visiting a bedridden patient, asked a neighbor whether anyone else had called. "Only that old woman who comes to scrub her floors," she was told. The "old woman" was Vincent, who arrived in the dim morning light in his habit to clean up and make tea for the invalid.

Wherever Vincent went he wore his habit; he did not possess a suit. Because he walked everywhere, Vincent attracted much attention from passing urchins, who were apt to shout "Gandhi" after him.

Though he could, and did, out-walk many a younger man, he did not walk merely to keep fit. A friend of Chesterton and Belloc, he sympathized strongly with the Distributist gospel of self-supporting rural existence and blamed the industrial revolution for driving men from God.

"My dear Parent," he wrote once in a magazine article, "never send your son to a school whose headmaster replies to you with a typewriter. The God of Abraham, Isaac, and Jacob cursed the men who put their trust in chariots and horses. What will be his attitude to a teacher who trusts in a *machine?* He may tell you that his school has an efficient system of central heating. So has hell!"

His large, handmade boots added to the eccentricity of his appearance; his handwoven habit he always washed himself, with much splashing but little success. Its blotches made many a woman long to get her hands on it.

Though he often said that he ate too much, Vincent's asceticism was formidable. Like Saint Dominic he never slept in bed, always on the floor, and he never sat down to read or write; he always stood or knelt. He firmly believed that most people wore too many clothes. "If you feel cold take something off — you'll feel warmer when you put it on again," he advised. Like some Tibetan monks, and like some of the saints, he seemed able to generate his own heat.

Some of his quips were worthy of Oscar Wilde: Hearing nuns' confessions was, he said, "like being nibbled to death by ducks." Yet throughout his life he retained a childlike simplicity and once tried to persuade a little girl to preach to him from the pulpit at Haverstock Hill. When she proved too shy to attempt a sermon, Vincent was genuinely disappointed. "I'm sure I should have learned much from you, dear child," he said as he helped her down.

A colleague, passing his door one night, heard him say: "Now, dear Lord, please go away. Brother Vincent wants to sleep."

He was businesslike in his approach to death; ever considerate of others, he worked hard at winding up his affairs. "I've found that dying is a full-time job," he told his Hyde Park audience with a smile.

Those who heard his final Hyde Park lecture never forgot his parting message: "Jesus Christ is love, love, love." His voice was very faint now, yet strangely it could be heard even at the edge of the large crowd.

Vincent McNabb, O.P., died on June 17, 1943. "I am sorry — he wasn't such a bad old stick," said one of his fiercest hecklers.

Ten years later, from that same platform on which he had spoken so often, one of his Dominican confreres asked Catholics in the audience to sign a petition for the opening of his cause.

6

"I HAVE PROMISES TO KEEP"

Dr. Tom Dooley

There was a good deal of banter as Tom Dooley climbed onto the operating table to have the lump on his chest removed. To his assistants, it seemed funny to see the great Dr. Dooley reduced to the rank of patient in his own hospital at Myong Sing in Laos.

It was only a minor operation, performed under a local anesthetic, so jokes seemed in order. The patient himself managed a wisecrack or two as his older colleague, Dr. William Van Vallin, skillfully went to work.

It was Bill Van Vallin, on a visit from the States, who suggested that the lump should come off. It had been giving Tom a good deal of pain, and both men thought that it was a sebaceous cyst. With the operation completed, Tom stared at the lump in surprise.

"Bill — it's jet black."

Dr. Van Vallin kept his professional calm.

"Yes, Tom," he replied. "It is."

The tumor was placed in formalin to be analyzed at a laboratory in Bangkok. Dr. Van Vallin left with it, and Tom Dooley went back to work. The lump, he now decided, was not a cyst but almost certainly a calcified blood clot from a fall he had suffered some time before.

In fact it was a malignant melanoma — a deadly form of cancer. Eighteen months later, on the day after his thirty-fourth birthday, Tom Dooley died in New York. Thousands filed past his coffin. A TV newscaster, attempting to cover the scene, broke down and wept.

"He had so little time, but how superbly he used it." The *New York Times* spoke for all the millions who admired him. At an age when most clever young doctors are only beginning to make their mark, Tom was internationally famous. People all over the world knew of his work for the stricken people of Southeast Asia. Medico, the organization he founded, brought medical aid to thousands who would otherwise have died without hope.

While he was alive, Tom had his critics. He was accused of arrogance, impatience. Some said fame had gone to his head. Others rejected these charges indignantly. Those who made them, they declared, did not know the real Tom Dooley.

Certainly Tom had no illusions about himself. He insisted that would-be recruits to Medico be warned that Dooley was a difficult fellow to work for. One of his friends told him: "If you are a saint, then you wear your halo at a mighty crooked angle." Needless to say, Tom never made any such claim — he would have laughed at the very idea. Yet today many who knew him are convinced that a saint is exactly what he was. Already the first stage in his cause has begun.

Thomas Anthony Dooley III was born in Saint Louis, Missouri, on January 17, 1927. His father, an engineer, was an executive of the American Car and Foundry Company. His mother, daughter of a Pennsylvania family, had been married previously to an Air Force pilot who was killed soon after World War I. The Dooleys divided their time between their home in Saint Louis and their six-roomed "cottage" at Green Lake, Wisconsin.

Tom's earliest talent was for music: He could read notes before he could read words and at four was already playing simple pieces on the piano. At school he showed a flare for languages, which stood him in good stead when he went to Asia.

But French was always the language he loved most. Aided by summer courses at the Sorbonne in Paris, he became fluent in it.

Tom Dooley was a clever young fellow, no doubt about that. He was good-looking, too, and he had plenty of charm. He drew girls like a magnet and could jitterbug formidably, flipping his partner over his back in a fashion rarely seen outside Hollywood. He was a dashing horseman.

It was his boundless energy and self-confidence that really made people notice him. He was overawed by nobody. When he was still a schoolboy, his mother worried that his enthusiastic collecting for charity might offend the neighbors, some of them eminent people. "Why, Mother," Tom replied, "they're really the same as everyone else, aren't they?"

When Tom announced that he wanted to be a doctor, his father opposed the idea, fearing that Tom might have too little patience to survive the years of grinding study. He also thought his son too artistic to be a medical man.

In the end Tom got his way, but first came a stint as a medical corpsman in the Navy, where he distinguished himself by persuading Hildegarde, a renowned nightclub singer, to visit his patients in the Navy Hospital at Saint Albans, Long Island. The lady insisted that Corpsman Dooley escort her through the wards — and escort her he did, with the bemused officers trailing along behind.

He loved the Navy so much that he decided to return to it once his studies at Notre Dame were complete. During his student years, Tom's impatience with the routine of classes and clinics did indeed sometimes bring him into collision with authority. However, he safely graduated from medical school in March 1953, and the following month began his internship in the naval hospital at Camp Pendleton, California.

Postings to Japan and the Philippines followed. Then, later in 1954, Tom was ordered to Vietnam to help in the transfer of the half-million refugees who chose exile in the South rather than life in the Communist North.

From his arrival in Japan, Tom had been fascinated with the Orient: its languages, its religions, its culture. Many of its values appealed to him deeply, especially the reverence shown to old age and the care older children gave younger ones. It hurt him when his patients, because he was an American, treated him with fear and suspicion; yet he understood why they felt that way. Experience had taught them to equate a white skin with colonialism and exploitation.

Soon, many were won over by Tom's happy, forceful personality and by his medical skill. Like the Pied Piper, he could charm a boatload of frightened orphans into gurgles of laughter as he joked with them in fluent Vietnamese. Many a little boy, successfully treated for an eye infection, would return bearing a smaller brother on his back for healing by the *Bac Sy My* (American doctor).

Tom was not merely treating starvation and disease. Many of his patients had suffered at the hands of the Vietminh. Among them were women, children, and old people, some of whom had been badly beaten up. Tom was himself arrested by the new Communist masters and held for a day and a night in a stinking cell while they questioned him with courteous venom about his rich American lifestyle: "Monsieur, is it not true that you own a car whose value equals the annual salary of many Vietnamese?"

Before that happened, however, he had seen for himself what these self-appointed champions of the poor were capable of doing to their fellow man.

Late one November night, Tom was awakened at his hotel by a Vietnamese priest who asked him to see a patient urgently. Together the two men drove in a jeep to the outskirts of the city.

After many months of caring for his refugees, Tom was used to heartrending sights. Nevertheless, the spectacle that now met his eyes filled him with horror.

The patient, an elderly priest in a Communist-held village, had been in his church when the Vietminh soldiers burst in and accused him of preaching lies about them. The priest told them that he spoke only of God.

The Communists took the old man, hung him from a beam by his feet and stripped him naked. They beat him with short bamboo rods, covering almost every inch and attacking the most sensitive areas with particular savagery. They rammed chopsticks deep into his ears and dug thorns deep into his head, in mockery of Christ's suffering. When the altar servers arrived in the morning, he was still hanging there. The blood vessels in his eyes had ruptured, leaving him nearly blind.

The youngsters knew that if the Vietminh returned, the priest would certainly be killed, that they had to get him away. With incredible bravery and resourcefulness, they carried the injured priest through the rice paddies to the river's edge, a journey lasting a day and a night. They dared not try to take him across the river in daylight, so they hid among the rushes until nightfall. Then they put the stretcher on a wooden raft, pushed the raft across the fast-flowing current to the opposite bank, and carried the priest to the mission where the doctor found him. Amazingly, he recovered — thanks to Tom's care.

Another of his priest patients had suffered even more cruelly. Not only had the Vietminh destroyed his hearing, they had cut out his tongue with a rusty bayonet so he could never again preach the Word of God. With him were a group of children whom he had been teaching. Their eardrums, too, had been pierced so that they would never again hear it. Yet another priest had six nails driven into his head.

"Why are these atrocity cases always priests?" Tom asked later. "Why do they hate priests so? Is it because they are so near the One they really hate?"

One of his last acts before leaving Vietnam was to rescue a five-foot statue of Our Lady of Fatima that stood above the altar of a church in Haiphong. Many years before, it had been the pope's gift to a group of Vietnamese pilgrims in Rome. Tom was determined that it should not fall into Communist hands. The poor, barefoot clergy sadly agreed to let him carry it to safety.

For his services to the refugees, Tom was personally decorated by South Vietnam's President Diem. His own country awarded him the Legion of Merit. Yet whatever Tom had done for the refugees, he felt that they had done much more for him. They had shown him where his life's work lay.

Once, he had dreamed of becoming a fashionable obstetrician. Later on he imagined himself as surgeon general of the Navy. Others, including the reigning surgeon general, also saw Tom as a future occupant of that post. Now all such ambitions were abandoned as Tom began to dream of a future devoted to the suffering people of Southeast Asia.

On leave in Washington, he attended a party at the South Vietnamese Embassy. There he talked to his hosts about his plan for a small medical mission, independent of all governmental or political ties, to work in areas where there was no doctor. Diplomats from Cambodia and Laos were among the guests, and Tom, as he talked, noticed that the Laotian ambassador was following him keenly.

"Dr. Dooley," the ambassador asked, "why should you, a young man with your career before you, offer to make so great a sacrifice?"

Into Tom's mind came the words of a naval corpsman in Haiphong. Questioned about American motives, he answered:

"We just want to do what we can for people who ain't got it so good."

The simple words touched the ambassador deeply. A few days later Tom told his mother: "I'm resigning from the Navy and I'm going to Laos."

Some of Tom's friends, people who thought they knew him well, were astonished by his decision. Even his mother admitted that she was shocked. Yet she, above all others, knew the sense of responsibility Tom had always felt toward his fellow man. The whole family had been deeply affected by the death of Tom's older brother, Earle, in World War II. Before he was killed by a mortar shell, Earle had written a letter to his family charging them to do all in their power to fight against war and the things that led to war. Tom carried that letter constantly.

His deepest motivation, however, came from his faith. Tom was a patriotic American, and he wanted those whom he helped to think well of his country. Yet that help, he insisted again and again, must be without strings, political or religious. He did not seek to turn his patients into Republicans or Democrats, nor did he try to make them Catholics. He brought Christ to them, not by preaching but by devoting his life to their care.

Operation Laos, as Tom called his mission, began in July 1956 at a village called Van Vieng, where he and his three ex-Navy helpers arrived covered in mud and red dust, looking like men in dire need of help rather than men come to give it. "For the man who had never seen an American," Tom recalled later, "we must have been something of a disenchantment."

Nevertheless the villagers gave him a warm welcome, and even the children pitched in to help them to prepare a hut standing on five-foot stilts as their living quarters. While washing and painting proceeded, the village livestock — pigs, cows, chickens, and ducks — scratched about underneath.

The hospital, where twenty-five patients lay on mats, was housed in a dispensary owned by the Laotian government. Many more patients were treated in their own homes for malaria, pneumonia, malnutrition, and beri-beri.

From the beginning the International Rescue Commission took Operation Laos under its wing, and Tom's energetic begging brought supplies from America's leading pharmaceutical companies. Walt Disney donated a projector and a collection of his own films, which proved invaluable in winning the confidence of youngsters.

Of Tom's hundreds of outpatients, many walked vast distances to relate their symptoms and to receive medicines, not from Tom himself but from the Lao assistants whom he had trained as dispensers. For Tom was more than a doctor, he was also an educator, and the American doctors who joined him were expected to fill the same role. "An Asian helping an Asian is better than an American helping an Asian," he would declare firmly, as he watched his pupils learn their basic skills. Many quickly reached a high degree of proficiency, rudimentary though their training was. Midwives qualified when they had assisted at twenty-five deliveries and completed a two-month course.

To the charge that he was practicing nineteenth-century medicine, he pleaded guilty. Once he left, he told his critics cheerfully, his pupils might well revert to eighteenth-century medicine, but even that would be a gain for people who were living in the fifteenth century. Meanwhile, he would listen with a mixture of pride and amusement as young men who, a few months previously, did not know one end of a hypodermic from the other, discussed patients' symptoms with the aplomb of Mayo Clinic physicians.

Some of those symptoms were horrible enough, although familiar to the Lao helpers, who had grown up with the effects of starvation and disease all around them.

One day, for example, a group arrived at the clinic after a hundred-mile walk, bringing with them a sickly-looking young mother who thrust a bundle of clothing under their noses. As Tom and his assistants unwrapped the many layers, they found a child whose abdomen was so huge and distended that it looked as though it might burst at any moment, like an overblown balloon. Around the child's navel were a dozen or so marks where a witch doctor had burned the skin with pieces of gingerroot to draw out the sickness. Herself ill, the mother had been unable to nurse the child, so she fed it rice and water. Soon, it developed beri-beri.

Even after Tom's arrival, the power of the witch doctors remained great, for the beliefs of centuries are not upset in a day. Tom soon learned to treat them as professional colleagues. When he called he would first gravely stir the pot in which the all-powerful potation, liberally seasoned with incantations, was bubbling. Having thus established a rapport, he would settle himself to discuss the patient's condition. It was tacitly agreed that any credit for a cure must be equally shared between Eastern and Western medicine. Any eggs or other produce received by way of fees were similarly divided.

This policy of cooperation paid a hundredfold dividend. Frequently Tom would be called when the witch doctor had failed, sometimes at short notice. Once he arrived by jeep, having been awakened at 3 a.m., to find a man in his early forties close to death from pneumonia. Tom put him on an improvised stretcher, raised the lower part of his body, and constructed a crude vaporizer from a firepot, an old blanket, and a length of bamboo attached to a teakettle. "That was nineteenth-century medicine all right," said one of his helpers, "but it saved the man's life."

Even though he had to work in primitive conditions, Tom would tolerate no relaxation of standards in any of his hospitals.

No matter how trying the circumstances, maximum hygiene had to be observed. An American assistant who arrived in the operating theater minus cap and gown got a sharp dressing-down, even though he felt he had a legitimate excuse. Soon afterward, Tom presented him with a length of material and told him to have a cap and gown made forthwith.

Episodes like this naturally helped give Tom a reputation for arrogance. The truth was that he had no patience with lax-ity, or anything that seemed like it. That his style was autocratic cannot be denied; no doubt his service background was largely responsible for that. "You must give the orders and they must obey," he told an American colleague whom he thought too much inclined to consult his subordinates.

Demanding total self-sacrifice from himself, he also demanded it from others. "If there are any emergency calls in the night, I'll wake you and you can drive me," he told another helper. As the man wryly observed later: "It would never occur to him to *ask*."

Yet with his patients he was always the soul of courtesy. An elderly whisky seller, whom Tom had treated for tuberculosis, spotted Tom and an American colleague as they walked through the marketplace. Tom stopped to chat, and the old man offered each of them a drink of his unspeakable local brew from a com-mon cup, which must have been full of disease-laden bacteria.

Tom, whose favorite drink was bourbon, drank without flickering an eyelid and thanked the donor politely. When his companion queasily tried to decline the liquor, Tom dug him in the ribs.

"Drink it, you fool!" he hissed. "You can't offend his hospi-tality!"

When he established Medico in 1956, Tom was already famous, thanks to his published account of the Vietnamese evacuation, *Deliver Us From Evil*. He received thousands of letters from well-wishers, especially after *Reader's Digest* ran a condensation. As his fame grew, discussion of Tom's shortcomings, real or alleged, became public — part of his cross during the few years that were left to him.

Those who called him a self-glorifying phony hurt him deeply. Because he was so forceful, few realized that he was also a deeply sensitive man.

"What do you get out of this deal, Dooley?" a brash reporter asked him.

"Plenty," Tom replied evenly. "My life is more worthwhile."

Tom *was* an unabashed publicity-seeker, not because he wanted people to admire him, but because he knew that the books, lecture tours, and news stories brought him the dollars and the volunteers that Medico needed. Yet he recoiled from any attempt to put him on a pedestal.

"People keep trying to make me into a Saint Francis," he growled once. "It's gotten so that I can't walk into a bar and have a beer."

When villagers kowtowed to him on the roads of Laos, he would immediately raise them up.

"Don't worship me or anyone else — worship God," he would tell them. "You're as good as I am. You're as good as anyone in the world."

He grew really cross when Medico's New York headquarters proposed that he have his own personally headed notepaper. "Whoever thought that one up should go and stand in the corner," he snorted. "I don't care how you people in New York use my name, so long as you are sure it helps Medico. But let's not get silly."

Medico grew naturally out of Tom's work at Van Vieng. As support gathered in volume, it became possible to realize his dream of an organization that would send medical teams such as his own to deprived areas throughout the world.

Conscious of his own limitations, Tom did not make himself Medico's administrative head. Anyway, he wanted to remain in Laos. Dr. Peter Comanduras, a medical man with the right kind of experience, was appointed to run Medico in New York, and an advisory board of distinguished doctors was set up.

Among those who sent their good wishes was Dr. Albert Schweitzer, who had done much to inspire Tom originally. A short time before, he had visited Schweitzer at his hospital in Lamberené.

With Medico safely launched, Tom returned with a glad heart to Laos. He based himself now at Muong Sing, in the far north of the country, where Laos, China, and Burma (now Myanmar) meet. Though Medico opened other hospitals in Laos, Muong Sing was the one he made his own. Already the Chinese radio stations were broadcasting regular denunciations of Dooley, the capitalist agent, but Tom did not worry about that. Instead he rejoiced in the name his patients gave him — *Than Mo America*. Literally, this means "Honorable Man of Medicine from America."

One of the Americans who joined him there, Earl Rhine, had a flair for dentistry. He got an even more colorful name: *Than Mo Chep Keo* — "Honorable Man of Medicine for Pain in Teeth."

Earl and his friend Dwight Davies left their young wives and their studies at the University of Texas to give Medico a piece of their lives. Despite his self-proclaimed faults, Tom attracted many other idealistic young people to his side. Most became personally devoted to him, as well as to the work.

The first encounter could be daunting. A young man who had never been east of Oklahoma might be summoned to meet Tom in a New York hotel the next day. That he had some prior commitment, or did not possess the fare, was not accepted as an excuse. When he was up against it in some jungle village, the youngster would need self-sacrifice and resourcefulness in plenty. If he got to the appointment on time, he had passed the first test.

Whether Tom saw the applicant personally or not, he always had his background checked out thoroughly. In particular, Tom was wary of taking on anyone whose motives might be suspect. One man he did interview was a young Catholic who, having realized that he did not have a vocation, had given up his studies for the priesthood.

With this candidate, Tom was almost cruel. He accused him of wanting to go to Asia so he could turn Buddhists into Catholics, and so compensate himself for not becoming a priest. So abrasive was the grilling that the young man grew white with anger. Nevertheless, he refused to lose his temper and stuck to his guns. His motive, he insisted, was the same as Tom's own. He simply wanted to help people who "ain't got it so good."

In fact the interview was simply another Dooley test. Having come through it with flying colors, the ex-seminarian was duly appointed to Medico. He proved a first-rate field worker.

When he made up his mind to accept someone, Tom did not waste time on formalities. "Okay, you leave next month," he would say. "You will work at — . Get a map and look it up."

Many of the volunteers were doctors or other health professionals. Some, like Earl and Dwight, went on to study medicine after completing their stint with Medico. For these, the work they were doing offered a range of experience far greater than they could ever have found at home. Leprosy and smallpox, diseases long banished from the West, were part of the everyday scene. Diphtheria, whooping-cough, and typhoid, well-known to earlier generations of United States doctors, were still alive and flourishing in the villages of Laos.

Intricate surgery was practiced in the humblest of operating rooms. More than once Tom had to perform plastic surgery on youngsters horribly disfigured in attacks from wild bears. One lad had his left eye and the bridge of his nose torn off. Tom had to do his best with the ribbons of flesh that were left.

Another small patient, similarly patched up, presented the surprised surgeon with a little dog as a token of his appreciation. Thanking him, Tom asked smilingly: "What can I do with it?"

It was the boy's turn to look surprised. "Eat it," he replied.

Though Tom enjoyed seeing his family on visits to the States, he was always eager to get back to his patients once the lectures had been delivered and the conferences with colleagues completed. Only in Laos was he completely happy.

In his book *The Night They Burned the Mountain*, Tom described how he first got the news of his fatal cancer. A soldier walked into the hospital at Muong Sing and announced that a telegram awaited him at the fortress. Because it had come via military radio, Tom's first thought was that it concerned the war. Communist troops were massing on the border, and some reports said they were already in Laos.

The telegram was from Peter Comanduras, Medico's director, recalling him to New York immediately. Even then Tom did not suspect that his own health was involved. Had something happened to his mother, he wondered? Or was there some crisis within Medico itself?

In Vientiane, on the journey home, someone suggested that he was required to appear in a TV show. If that proved true, Tom replied, he would use language on-air that would close the station down forever. War casualties might arrive in Muong Sing at any moment. Didn't Peter Comanduras realize that his place was in his hospital?

In fact, Tom's closest associates already knew the truth. One of them broke it to him as he passed through Bangkok. The words, said Tom, made no impact on him whatever. They entered his head like a fist jammed into a pillow.

When Tom landed in New York and phoned his mother with the news, she also could not absorb it. She felt confident that with rest and care, her son would be well again soon.

Around his neck, Tom had for some years worn a Saint Christopher medal engraved with some lines from *Stopping by Woods on a Snowy Evening*, the well-known poem by Robert Frost:

The woods are lovely, dark and deep,
But I have promises to keep
And miles to go before I sleep.

Upon these words he had built his life. Now they had a magnificent urgency. He set himself to live them as never before.

Far from giving in to his condition, he redoubled his activities, flying around the world to extend the work of Medico to as many places as possible as well as caring for his patients in Laos.

First, however, Tom had a task to perform in New York. He had reacted acidly when his friend in Vientiane suggested that he was to appear on TV. Yet now he *did* appear on TV, in a program that made history. For the first time, millions of viewers heard a cancer patient talk about his operation — and then they saw him having it.

By the time the program was screened, on April 21, 1960, Tom was back in Southeast Asia. In his room at Memorial Hospital, he admitted to the CBS reporter, Howard K. Smith, that his condition caused him some discomfort — he rejected the word "pain" as being too strong. When Smith suggested that he was treating his situation in a way that was almost blithe, Tom replied: "I don't want any of that 'dying doctor's agony' stuff. That's stupid."

He welcomed the cameras, he explained, because in America there was a great deal of ignorance about cancer: the same sort of ignorance that existed in his village in Laos. Patients were crippled by fear before they ever got into a hospital, and that fear handicapped their treatment from the start. He wanted to make people see that they need not be so afraid of cancer as they had been in the past.

Tom spoke to the camera as fluently and encouragingly as though it were a patient in Muong Sing, reaching out especially to people who might be suffering like himself. As one of the TV technicians put it, he was a "natural."

The viewers saw two operations. The first, which was exploratory, showed that the cancer had not spread as far as had been feared. In the second, the surgeons cut out the cancerous tissue. So far as it went this operation was successful, and Tom left the hospital ten days later. But he knew, as did others, that the cancer could already be spreading through his bloodstream and growing in tiny spots in his lungs or liver, or in other vital organs. In fact, that was what happened.

Meanwhile, Tom had his promises to keep. No sooner was he back on his feet than he set off around America on a fund-raising tour. The audiences who listened to him soon found that illness had done little to dent his humor. In Saint Louis, his hometown, he had doctors roaring with laughter at his sly comparison of the noncommittal grunts of a Lao witch doctor and those of an American consultant, when faced with a patient whose condition they could not diagnose.

Christmas found him loaded with gifts, back at Muong Sing. Every one of the village children got his own individually wrapped present. Tom was happy to find everybody safe and sound. During his absence in the States, he had feared that the Communists might overrun the hospital, for he knew the likely fate of any of his colleagues whom they caught. The Americans would be publicly beheaded; the Lao workers would be hacked to death.

On New Year's Eve, he wrote Peter Comanduras in New York: "I feel okay, but I know I'm not the same Dooley I was a year ago . . ." A young doctor must be found, he said, to take over at Muong Sing in case he himself could not return after his next medical checkup in May.

The checkup, when it came, gave no indication that the melanoma was still present and this, coupled with Tom's amazing energy, gave some people false hopes. Even some of his doctor friends let themselves believe he had the cancer beaten. Tom himself indulged in no such wishful thinking. He knew full well that a satisfactory report, so soon after his operation, meant little.

During 1960 he visited Burma, Vietnam, Afghanistan, Malaya (now Malaysia), Hong Kong, and Cambodia. In each country he did the groundwork for new Medico projects. He journeyed to Teheran and to several European capitals as well — London, Paris, and Rome. At a private audience, Pope John XXIII emptied his desk drawer of medals and rosaries and gave them to the dying young American of whom he had heard so much. In Rome, also, he was made a member of the Oblates of Mary Immaculate — a rare honor for a layman.

"If this guy's ill I'd sure hate to follow him around when he's well," said one of his companions on the tour. And indeed, his energy seemed inexhaustible.

Back in the States, he received an honorary degree from his own university, Notre Dame. Among others being honored that day was President Dwight D. Eisenhower.

As they donned their robes in the locker room, Tom asked Ike to give his brother Malcolm a lift back to New York on board the presidential plane. Malcolm was, he explained, an executive at Medico's New York headquarters, a busy man who had to get back to his desk. In fact this was pure Dooley chutz-pah — Tom really wanted Malcolm to be able to tell his grandchildren about the day he flew home with the president. Ike readily obliged, and an astonished Malcolm Dooley found himself being whisked away by secret servicemen and hustled into a car in the motorcade.

The time came, however, when Tom could no longer keep up his façade of high spirits. Forced to rest in a Hong Kong hospital, he looked at his X-ray plates and saw that the cancer had spread to his spine. "And I still have so much to do!" he lamented.

He returned once more to Muong Sing, but he was not to see another Christmas there. Christmas Day 1960 found him in Bangkok, lying racked with pain on a mattress on the floor of his hotel room. He badly wanted to go to Midnight Mass at Holy Redeemer Church, but was too ill to make it. So Redemptorist Father John Boucher brought him Holy Communion instead.

When news of Tom's illness broke, one of his friends remarked bitterly: "There are thousands of jerks in the world we could do without. Why does someone like Tom Dooley have to get cancer?"

Yet this was never Tom's attitude. He did not complain, or ask: "Why me?" As he lay in his hotel room on that Christmas Day, he told Father Boucher: "If this is the way God wants it to be, this is the way I want it too." His suffering, he was convinced, had been sent for a purpose.

During the journey from the airport to Memorial Hospital in New York, he asked Teresa Gallagher, a devoted aide, to remind him to write and thank a stewardess who had been kind to him on the last, agonizing leg of the flight, when he could neither stand, sit, nor lie down without pain.

On Tuesday, January 17, his birthday, Cardinal Spellman visited him in Room 910 — the room from which he had made his TV appearance. Though sinking fast, Tom recognized the cardinal and rose up in bed to make the Lao sign of greeting, head bowed and hands clasped before his face.

The cardinal left the room with tears in his eyes. "I tried to assure him that in his thirty-four years, he had done what very few have done in the allotted scriptural lifetime," he said.

At 9:45 p.m. the next day, Tom Dooley died peacefully, his promises kept.

7

"IT IS CONSTANCY THAT GOD WANTS"

Venerable Matt Talbot

On a breezy morning in 1925, an elderly Dubliner collapsed in Granby Lane as he made his way to Mass at the Dominican church. A woman and her son came running from their home and tried to carry him inside, but the frail body proved surprisingly heavy. When a priest in his black-and-white habit hurried from the church to kneel beside him, the old man was still lying on the pavement.

He was dead — the priest knew it, as he spoke the absolution. The bystanders knew it too, as they murmured their own prayers. The lined face had a sweet, serene look. Had he known he was dying, even as he clutched instinctively at the wall? At any rate death had not frightened him; a look at him would tell anyone that. But his clothes . . . his clothes moved everyone to pity. What kind of poor beggar, even in July, went around in such thin old rags?

In the hospital mortuary a Sister of Mercy, preparing the body for burial, cut through those rags with her scissors. Suddenly, she found herself snipping at solid metal. Now she knew why the old fellow had been so hard to lift. Around his waist was a heavy iron chain, its links rusted into his flesh. There were more chains around his arm and his leg, each of them rusted like the first.

Who was the old man? For several hours nobody knew. When he was identified, the details were sparse. Matthew

Talbot, aged sixty-nine, storekeeper for a timber firm, lived alone in a rear tenement in Upper Rutland Street. Just another lonely old Dublin bachelor, gone to his reward. But the chains . . . dear God, why did he carry those around, punishing his worn-out body so cruelly? Was he, perhaps, a little bit mad?

There was nothing mad about Matt Talbot — the few people who knew him soon made that clear. To his workmates at the dockside timber yard, he was renowned in about equal parts for his common sense, his quiet piety, and the ancient derby that he constantly wore jammed down over his bald head.

The derby was more than a head covering. It was also a weapon against the blasphemy he heard all too often from the rough-and-ready dock workers. Whenever a man took the Lord's name in vain, off would come the hat in reparation. It came off no matter how often the offense was repeated — and there were men who deliberately tried to tire Matt's arm. Happily, there were others who learned to curb their tongues, at least when Matt was around.

When the Angelus rang, the hat would come off again, and Matt would recite the prayer, ignoring the jeers of the irreverent.

He was at his happiest with the children of the yard's lodge-keeper. During slack moments he would amuse them with stories of his favorite saints, and at Christmastime he always had a store of small coins, which he would at first pretend he had lost. A frantic search would follow, until he triumphantly produced the coins from his ragged pockets and pressed them into eager little hands.

No, Matt was not mad. A little eccentric, maybe, but a good man whose religion was more than outward show; a man ready to help someone in need.

Had anyone told them that for sixteen years of his life Matt was a hopeless drunkard, most of them would have been surprised. Had they been able to foresee the future, they would have been more surprised still.

Matt was only twelve when he first came home drunk. The hiding that he got from his hardworking father did nothing to cure him. Already he had left school and was earning a few shillings a week as a messenger for a firm of wine merchants and Guinness-bottlers. It was not just the boozy atmosphere that led young Matt astray. Like many other Irish workmen of the time, he was a victim of the evil system whereby wages were paid in "checks" cashable in some local bar. The foreman took a rake-off from the barkeeper, and a man who failed to collect the proper proportion of his pay in drinks might soon find himself out of a job.

Although Matt's father found work for him elsewhere, the damage was done. Still a teenager, Matt was already a confirmed alcoholic who would gladly sweep the barroom floor to earn a free pint of beer. Week in, week out, his entire pay went for beer. In his sixteen years of hitting the bottle, his mother received toward her son's keep the grand total of one shilling — roughly equal to twenty cents.

Though permanently fuddled, Matt was never nasty in his cups — all his drinking companions later testified to that. Another trait everyone remembered: Though Matt frequently had to listen to dirty jokes, he never told them. He was generous to the ultimate degree; when Matt had money, everybody drank. It never worried him that he had paid for the last round, and for the one before that. Surely, if he was broke, would not his friends be just as ready to treat him?

No, they would not — as Matt discovered for himself one unforgettable morning in 1884. Getting up without a cent in his pocket, he waited hopefully on the street corner for a barroom buddy to offer him the liquor his body craved. One by one they passed him by; some of them, quite literally, on the other side.

So this was it, he thought bitterly, as he turned his steps homeward. This was what it amounted to, the spurious friendship of the tavern! Each of those men knew what he was suffering, knew he was broke. Each knew that, had their situations been reversed, he would never have walked by and left them parched. Yet in their own determination to drink as much as possible, they had ignored his need.

He thought with shame of the cruel trick he had once played on a poor fiddler who toured the pubs playing for a few pence. When the man's back was turned, Matt slipped out and pawned his fiddle to buy everyone another round of drinks. Next day he tried to redeem the fiddle, but he didn't have the money. He never saw the fiddler again. Then and there, Matt Talbot came to a decision. If this was what alcohol did to men, he would have no more of it. He would sign the pledge.

Had anyone told him an hour before that he would even contemplate such a step, he would have said it was crazy. His friends, when they saw him drinking mineral water, could not believe their eyes. Matt Talbot, teetotaler; it simply was not possible. Nobody believed that he would keep the pledge — not his friends, not his parents, certainly not Matt himself. Mistrusting his own resolve, he signed it for three months. He kept it for forty-one years. He never touched alcohol again.

Nobody helped Matt through his terrible withdrawal symptoms. No nursing home dried him out, no friend from Alcoholics Anonymous came in answer to his call — that splendid institution had not yet been invented. Poor Matt had only his own willpower to see him through; that and the grace of God.

When he said goodbye to drink, he stuck two crossed pins in his sleeve to remind him to pray without ceasing. They were still there when he died.

One terrible Sunday morning he tried several times to go to Holy Communion, but each time he felt himself driven back, convinced that he was about to lapse into his old ways. Wandering about Dublin, tormented by his craving for drink, he eventually collapsed outside the Jesuit church. There he lay prostrate, praying to God to relieve his agony, while disgusted worshipers stepped round him. They thought he was drunk.

It has been suggested that Matt's withdrawal symptoms never ceased; that his body continued to lust for alcohol until the day he died. It may have been true. Certainly, from the moment he signed the pledge, he subjected himself to penances that would have earned nods of approval from the sternest of the Desert Fathers.

Only on Sundays did he eat a decent meal. During the rest of the week his diet was mainly black tea and bread. At work his lunchtime "brew" was a nauseating mixture of cocoa and a pinch of tea, which he allowed to go tepid before he drank it.

He slept for only three-and-a-half hours each night. Bedtime was at ten-thirty; at two in the morning he was up again for a couple of hours' prayer before he went out to an early Mass. He would generally arrive at the church two hours before Mass time, waiting on the step for the door to open as he had once waited outside the pub.

He slit the knees of his pants so that when he prayed they were bare against the church kneelers and the floorboards of his room. Often he knelt on clinkers, lest bare boards should prove too comfortable.

No doubt Matt performed these penances in reparation for his own sins and for the sins of others. But if the craving for drink did indeed dog him to the end, then clearly he had an added motive. Only by such drastic means could he be sure of keeping his body in subjection, of arming himself against the temptation that wafted at him daily from the door of every pub.

One characteristic he did retain from his barroom days: He remained as generous as ever. But now, instead of scattering his money on drinks, he sent every penny to the missions, or gave it to the local clergy for the Dublin poor.

It was in order to send money to the missions that Matt wrote his one and only letter, just seven months before his death. He sent it to the friend who usually forwarded his donations for him, and it consisted of these few lines:

> Matt Talbot have Done no work for past 18 months i have been sick and Given over by Priest and Doctor i don't think i will work any more there one Pound from me and ten shillings from my Sister.

Writing letters, you will gather, did not come easily to Matt Talbot. His schooling had been of the briefest. Yet after his death, his room was found to contain the works of John Henry Newman, François-Louis Blosius, Pierre-Julien Eymard, Jean N. Grou, and other profound spiritual writers; and his laboriously copied notes showed that he had read them intelligently.

His principal inspiration was Saint Louis de Montfort. Under his influence, Matt began to wear the chains, which were the symbol of his slavery to Mary. The chains increased in weight as the years went by.

Occasionally he himself gave spiritual advice, sometimes with a sort of holy gruffness. When a woman complained that her brother, who had emigrated to America, was feeling lonely there, Matt nearly exploded.

"Lonely?" he demanded. "How can anyone be lonely, with our Lord always there in the tabernacle where anyone can visit Him?"

A friend who let bad weather keep him from daily Mass got a succinct Talbot rebuke: "It is constancy that God wants."

There was, you will be surprised to learn, one brief romantic episode in Matt's life. It happened not long after he had taken the pledge.

At this time he was working for a building firm, and the job took him to the home of a Protestant minister. The cook, a Catholic, took a fancy to the shy, politely spoken young man. Realizing that she would wait forever before he proposed to her, she took the initiative and popped the question herself.

"Don't be worrying about money," she told him. "I've enough saved for the both of us."

Matt, much taken aback, promised to make a novena to Our Lady and to give her his answer at the end of it. Nine days later he informed his suitor, with suitable expressions of regret, that Our Lady did not wish him to marry.

The cook, whether she knew it or not, had a lucky escape. Life with Matt would have been grueling indeed!

Though he became a Franciscan tertiary, he never seems to have felt a vocation to the religious life. He was content to remain in the world but not of it, living his fierce asceticism amid the poverty and turmoil in the Ireland of his day.

When Dublin bosses tried to break the unions, and the city's workers called a general strike, Matt came out with the rest. But he refused to join a picket line, and nobody held it against him.

He lived through the Troubles but never murmured against the English, even when they arrested him and made him stand, hands above his head, waiting to be searched. That happened after the blowing up of the North Wall Hotel, when people nearby were rounded up en masse. Matt and his workmates were quickly released.

In 1923 came Matt's long illness; his heart had weakened under the strain of his hard life. As his letter shows, he continued to think of the missions even as he lay on his back in a hospital, saving money for them from his modest sickness benefit payments. The ten shillings from his sister in fact came from him. It was his way of thanking her for taking care of him.

Contrary to his own expectation, he did return to work in the timber yard, but only briefly. Three months later he stepped from Granby Lane into eternity.

On June 29, 1952, Matt's body was exhumed from the humble grave in Glasnevin Cemetery. In the presence of the archbishop of Dublin, the president of Ireland, and numerous other dignitaries, the remains were formally examined — a necessary part of the canonization process. Afterward they were sealed into a new oak coffin and placed in a splendid vault, where his devotees come by the hundreds to pay their respects to the little man in the battered derby who is now a servant of God.

In a way Matt was lucky — luckier than most of us. He had to be a drunkard, or he had to be a saint. For him there was no middle way, no comfortable mediocrity. That option was simply not open to him.

In Matt's day it was poverty that drove people to drink. Prosperity, we have discovered, can have the same effect. All alcoholics, whether rich or poor, need prayers, and generous Matt must have said many for his fellow sufferers. No doubt he does so still. If and when he is canonized, alcoholics will have a powerful patron.

8.

"DON'T STOP PRAYING"

Blessed Brother André

*D*uring the first days of 1937, thousands of Canadians waited anxiously by their radio sets for news of a small, gray-haired man who lay dying peacefully in a Montreal hospital. The patient was not a statesman or a film star, but a humble lay brother of the Holy Cross Congregation who had spent much of his long life working as a porter at the College of Notre Dame.

For two days before his death he was in a coma, unaware of the long procession of men, women, and children who passed by his bed. Many of them were sick or lame, and all of them touched his hands with a medal or some other pious object.

Had Brother André known what was happening, he might not have been pleased, for he always reacted indignantly if he suspected that he was being treated as a saint. During his later years, he complained loudly when he discovered that some of his brethren were hoarding his cast-off clothing for relics. From then on, he counted his laundry carefully!

Whether or not Brother André was a saint, the Church will decide in due course — he was beatified in 1982. The undeniable truth is that for more than forty years, great crowds of the ill and the crippled came to his little room to be cured, and many of them were. Even without these apparent miracles, his deep holiness of life would have made him a candidate for sainthood.

Brother André was ninety-one when he died, but when little Alfred Bessette was born on August 9, 1845, few would have prophesied such a long life. From infancy he was a sickly child, a source of anxiety to his mother, Clothilde.

Isaac Bessette, a poor carpenter, lived with his large family at Saint Gregoire d'Iberville in the backwoods of Quebec. Their home was little better than a shack.

When Alfred was three, his father was killed by a falling tree. Nine years later his mother died of tuberculosis. The orphaned children were divided among their relatives, Alfred being taken in by an aunt and uncle at Saint-Césaire.

Apprenticed first to a shoemaker, then to a baker, Alfred proved too frail to follow either trade. During her anxious vigils beside his cradle, Clothilde Bessette had often prayed to Saint Joseph, Quebec's first patron, for her child. Now Alfred himself prayed that Saint Joseph would find him some work that he could do.

Even when he was small, Alfred had been a child of exceptional fervor: His brothers and sisters could not fail to notice how long and ardent were his prayers. As he grew up, he began to inflict severe penances upon himself. His horrified aunt found that, like Matt Talbot, he regularly wore a heavy chain around his waist under his clothes. Instead of sleeping in bed, he slept on the floor.

Like many other young Canadians, Alfred heard with wonder of the plentiful work and good wages to be found across the border in the United States. When a friend who had emigrated found him a job in a cotton mill at Plainfield, Connecticut, it appeared that Saint Joseph had answered his prayers. But after three years, Alfred had to come home again. Once more, his poor health had let him down.

Shortly before he left for Connecticut, Alfred had a strange dream, in which he saw Saint Joseph and then a magnificent stone church in a setting he did not recognize. Now, back in

Saint-Césaire, he began to think seriously about entering the religious life.

On the face of it, this seemed like a crazy ambition. Alfred had proved physically unfit for every secular occupation he had tried, and religious orders do not readily take on recruits who are likely to become invalids.

But when the young man confided his hopes to Saint-Césaire's parish priest, he received no discouragement. Father Provençal knew that here was someone with qualities beyond the ordinary. Because sickness had interfered with his schooling, Alfred had never learned to read or write, so the priest himself dispatched a letter to the Holy Cross Brothers. "I am sending you a saint for your congregation," he announced.

Despite this eyebrow-raising introduction, the brothers were skeptical. A frail, illiterate young fellow of twenty-five — it really did seem ridiculous to entertain him as a candidate. Two brothers traveled to Saint-Césaire with every intention of turning Alfred down gently. But when they came face-to-face with the small, intense young man, they were overwhelmed — especially by his burning devotion to Saint Joseph. "I'm sure that if I were allowed to enter his service my health would improve," he declared. Somewhat to their own astonishment, the bemused brothers found themselves recommending that Alfred be accepted.

And so, in the fall of 1870, Alfred Bessette came to the Holy Cross novitiate at Côte-des-Neiges, on the slopes of Mount Royal — the mountain that gave its name to the city of Montreal. Despite his poor health Alfred had always been a happy character, and now he was happier than ever before. The humblest, dreariest tasks brought him joy: Scrubbing, mending, washing dishes, all of these he did with the same cheerful smile. Within months he was given the longed-for habit and became a novice, Brother André.

Not for another two years could he become a full-fledged member of the congregation. The year that followed brought little sign that he was becoming stronger. His superiors began to wonder whether they had made a mistake. Because God had not sent him the necessary health, maybe Brother André ought not to be a religious after all.

When Bishop Bourget visited the brothers, Brother André seized his chance and made a direct appeal. Once again his shining fervor won the day. He was allowed to make his temporary vows and then, in 1872, his solemn profession. "After all," said his novice master, "even if he becomes unable to work, he can at least pray for us."

This "frail" brother worked and prayed with a vigor that would have taxed the strength of a giant — and continued to do so for the next sixty years. Sometimes he stayed up all night to pray or to complete his tasks, for in addition to his normal duties, he would often leave the Notre Dame College to visit local people who were sick or in trouble. He hardly ate anything; a piece of bread dipped in milk and water was his idea of a square meal.

By this time he was no longer illiterate: The brothers had taught him to read and write. He could not become a teacher — his education would never rise to those heights — yet his personality drew the boys like a magnet. Homesick newcomers, invited into his little office for a chat, would soon leave it all smiles.

Two small incidents increased his popularity and caused great wonder among his young friends. When a new football was needed, the boys were at first refused. Brother André told them to ask again and lo!, a new ball was given unto them. When, against all expectations, a picnic came by the same miraculous means, the boys were naturally agog to know how he did it.

"Don't thank me, thank Saint Joseph," was the answer, delivered with an enigmatic grin.

Soon more stories were circulating in and around the city. People said that when Brother André came to visit, the sick quickly got well. One day a crippled woman arrived at the college, helped along by two friends. She came upon a brother swabbing a corridor and asked to see Brother André.

"That's me," said the brother, straightening up.

"I have heard that you can cure sick people," she said. "Please, could you help me?"

Brother André smiled at her quizzically.

"Are you sure that you are crippled?" he asked. "I believe that you could walk on your own if you really tried. Why not go as far as the chapel and see?"

The friends who had been supporting her gingerly released their hold. Slowly and painfully, she limped off to the chapel. When she came back, she walked normally.

"When they told me you could heal, I didn't know whether to believe it or not," said the woman, her face tear-stained. "Now I know it's true."

"It isn't I who do the healing," Brother André told her. "It is Saint Joseph."

Still overcome with gratitude, the woman asked whether there was something she could do for her benefactor. The answer came as a surprise.

"You could pray that one day Saint Joseph will have a good home for his Son up there on the mountain," he smiled.

Many a time during the day, Brother André glanced up from his work at the tangle of trees and scrubland that covered the mountaintop. Often, in the evening, he climbed up there to pray.

Yet his dream of a church dedicated to Saint Joseph seemed wildly impractical. Neither the diocese nor his own congregation had any plans to build on the mountain, and anyhow someone else owned the land.

Nevertheless, Brother André continued to pray for a church. Not only did he pray, he began to save up. When the college pupils asked him to cut their hair, as they often did, he charged them five cents and put the money into a little jar, ready for the day when work would begin.

One day he buried a medal of Saint Joseph under a tree at the spot where, he firmly believed, the church would one day stand. In the following years, many other medals were buried there — tokens of gratitude from people who were cured through his prayers.

For his reputation as a miracle worker continued to grow, and some of his brethren became seriously concerned by the flow of pilgrims who came to seek his help. The lame walked straight, limbs threatened with amputation were saved, the blind were made to see.

Inevitably, the newspapers became interested in this humble lay brother who seemed able to work miracles, and the publicity proved embarrassing. Parents, suspecting some kind of chicanery, threatened to withdraw their sons from the college. There were those who openly called Brother André a quack.

Despite this hostility, both the provincial and the archbishop refused to interfere with his work for the sick. Both were convinced that he was a very holy religious indeed, and that his humility and his cheerful wisdom were a sufficient answer to his critics.

No doubt the backbiters would have been chastened had they known of the sinister persecution that the little Holy Cross brother had to suffer. For often, when he was at prayer, a big animal like a black cat manifested itself close to him. Books, glasses, plates, and other objects were thrown around the room. On one occasion the noise brought a colleague running.

Brother André was forced to admit that often, at his prayers, he was attacked by the forces of darkness.

When Brother André was a young man, Satan had assaulted him with terrible temptations of the flesh — he had rolled himself in the snow and done other severe penances to overcome them. Later, the temptations were more subtle. "Why should you be chosen to work these cures, Brother André?" a voice whispered. "Surely you must believe that you are a saint."

Brother André, of course, believed nothing of the kind. His cures, he continued to insist, were not really his at all: They were effected by God through the intercession of Saint Joseph. Countless times during his long life he hammered this message home. Yet, during the early years, the hostility persisted. First there were accusations of immodesty in his touching of sick people. There were even attempts to trap him. These having failed, he was reported to the Board of Health, who found nothing wrong and praised his sound common sense. In 1910 a still higher authority came down on his side: Pope (now Saint) Pius X sent a blessing. At last the critics were silenced.

The crowds of sufferers who came to Mount Royal found a kindly but brisk little man whose prescription, whatever the affliction, was always the same: "Rub yourself with the oil and medal of Saint Joseph. Make a novena and keep on praying to the saint."

As he stood behind the desk in his worn cassock, he rarely looked directly at the person to whom he spoke. Instead he looked somewhere beyond, as though seeing all the world's sufferings. The oil that he gave came from lamps that had burned before Saint Joseph's statue.

If, as sometimes happened, a cure was only partial, Brother André was in no way abashed. "Don't stop praying," he would say, "or you might lose what you have gained."

Once a woman asked his help because she was very tired. "Then pray for me," he asked, "for I, too, am very tired."

When tiredness got the better of him, he could be touchy. One Protestant woman was so upset by his manner that she left in tears. Not until some minutes later did she realize that her lameness had been cured.

He had little patience with those who *demanded* a cure. His reply to their "You must help me" was inevitably: "Why must I? Does God owe you anything? If you think so, you had better make your own arrangements with him."

If he knew that he had spoken unkindly, he was invariably sorry afterward. "But at least they have seen for themselves that I am just an ordinary sinner," he would console himself. "So long as they realize that it is Saint Joseph who works the cures, I don't mind if they think me a bad-tempered fellow."

Now and again there were incidents that brought his peasant humor to the fore. A woman whom he had observed robbing the college orchard appeared before him soon afterward to seek relief for her afflicted stomach. "Rub yourself with the oil of Saint Joseph," he told her dryly, "and eat fewer green apples."

He was deeply moved when a young woman came to seek help for her sister, who was very ill. He knew, without being told, that the girl herself had a serious heart condition.

"Why don't you ask for help for yourself, child?" he inquired gently.

"It doesn't matter about me," she replied. "It's for my sister that I have come."

Both sisters were soon made better.

Though he spent his life helping sufferers, he did not see suffering as necessarily evil. "We shouldn't always pray for miseries to be removed," he said. "Sometimes we should pray for strength to bear them better."

As we have seen, he could sometimes be less than kind. Yet with one type of client he showed endless patience and would spend an hour or more of his time. Those who had lapsed from the faith, or were hardened sinners, often left his presence reborn. "Oh, if you loved our dear Lord," he would tell them with tears in his eyes. "If you loved him as he loves you. If you realized how sin crucifies him again and again!"

His prescription for prayer was simple. "To pray well you must think of Jesus on the cross," he would say. "Surely you can see how impossible it is to be distracted when you think of your Brother crucified?"

Every night, no matter how exhausted, he would himself make the Stations of the Cross, slowly and with the utmost devotion.

As the fame of his cures spread, people came in increasing numbers to pray with him on the mountaintop. Despite all the obstacles standing in his way, Brother André never doubted that a church would be built up there, where God seemed so much closer. Sure enough, one by one, the obstacles were overcome.

First, the owner of the land unexpectedly came down in price, and the Holy Cross Congregation snapped it up. However, there was considerable reluctance to use it for a church, as this might look like recognition of a "cult" not approved by Rome.

One day in 1904, Brother André found himself a patient in the college infirmary. There was one other patient — his superior. Seizing the chance, Brother André pressed home the argument for a modest church to replace the little shrine he had already built there.

As usual, his fervor won the day. Work began in July. A mason who had been lame gave his services free in thanksgiving for his cure. At the edge of the building site stood a box for offerings. Somehow, there was always just enough money to pay the other workmen.

In November the church was dedicated; soon, it was decorated with the crutches of the cured. Though much enlarged during the next few years, it still proved too small. At Christmas 1916, a new Church of Saint Joseph was opened, with seats for a thousand worshipers and standing room for many more.

Once, when a substantial offering arrived in the mail, the little brother rubbed his hands and exclaimed: "Now we can build a bigger church."

His provincial, who was feeling a little edgy that day, snapped: "You'll be wanting a basilica next."

Then he looked up, and saw the faraway look in Brother André's eyes. . . .

In 1922 plans for a basilica were begun — the basilica that stands on Mount Royal today. This was the building that Brother André had seen in his dream so long before. He never saw it completed, for it was still without a roof when he died. But that did not worry him for, as a friend in New York pointed out: "You'll drop the roof on from heaven with your prayers."

During his later years he traveled much in the United States, the country where he had lived as a young man, and which he had never ceased to love. His fame always spread before him, though he never seemed to understand this. Once he told a friend: "I got into Jersey City just as they were holding a very fine procession — must have been some big local feast." He had failed to grasp that the procession was in his honor.

In the fall of 1931, he had a vision of the Sacred Heart, and then of Our Lady, holding the Infant Jesus. They appeared to him late at night, as he lay in bed.

Soon afterward, as he prayed in the church, a workman clearly saw Saint Joseph's statue shining in the darkness. Slowly it came toward Brother André as though on a cloud, and remained in front of him for about three minutes. The workman called out "Brother, Brother!" but Brother André seemed not to hear. Later he insisted that he had seen nothing unusual; he had been lost in prayer.

Until his final illness Brother André continued to practice a fierce asceticism, living chiefly on dry bread and strong coffee. "Eat as little as possible and pray as much as possible" was his prescription for a long life. Yet when he was entertained to dinner in New York, he amazed everyone by eating every course with apparent enjoyment.

As he grew old, he deplored what he saw as the immodesty of women's fashions, and he did not hesitate to make his views known. An offender was likely to be asked if she had come in a great hurry, as she had apparently forgotten to put on her dress.

After some initial hesitation, radio eventually won his blessing, mainly because it was a means of broadcasting religious services. But the greatest of God's new gifts, in Brother André's eyes, was the automobile. He loved riding in this splendid contraption, which went so much faster than the horse and buggy of his youth. More than one driver found himself eyeball-to-eyeball with the law, because his distinguished passenger had urged him beyond the speed limit. Usually, though, all was forgiven when the officer recognized the little figure grinning penitently in the back seat.

Today Brother André is buried in the crypt of the great basilica on Mount Royal, in a simple granite tomb that bears only his name. There the sick in body and soul visit him still, and just as in his lifetime, many go away cured.

9

"WHERE I SOW, OTHERS WILL REAP"

Venerable Charles de Foucauld

One October morning in 1886, a handsome young Frenchman went into the Church of Saint Augustin in Paris just as the nine o'clock Mass was beginning. He made for the confessional of the Abbé Huvelin and entered.

"Father, I haven't come to confession," he announced. "I lost my faith a long time ago."

"Then what may I do for you, my son?" The voice behind the grille was grave, yet serene.

"Instruct me. You see, I *want* to believe."

"Kneel down and make your confession," the priest commanded.

"But Father, I don't think you have understood . . ."

"Don't argue, my son. And don't worry. Just do as I say."

Still taken aback, the young man blurted out as many sins as he could remember. Having absolved him, the priest asked: "Now, are you fasting?"

"Yes," the penitent replied.

"Very well. Go straight away and receive Holy Communion." The penitent, an ex-army officer, knew an order when he heard one. Bemused, he went to the altar for the first time in twelve years.

In Saint Augustin a plaque commemorates that far-off morning when Charles de Foucauld came back to the Church.

It also records that, many years later, he said Mass there as a priest.

As most people know, Charles spent his life not in Paris but in the Sahara Desert. As a missionary he was not a success: He scarcely made a single convert. He tried to found a religious order and failed completely — his only novice soon left. When he died a martyr in 1916, the news caused scarcely a ripple. On the face of it his death was unnecessary, even ridiculous. His cousin, a general, described him as a fool.

Yet fifty years afterward, in his encyclical *Populorum Progressio*, Pope Paul VI held him up as an example to the world: a man who, by living the Gospel literally, earned for himself the title he claimed — Universal Brother.

Charles Eugene, Vicomte de Foucauld, was born in the beautiful old city of Strasbourg on September 15, 1858. When he was six his parents died within months of each other. Nevertheless he and his younger sister, Marie, had a happy childhood in the care of Colonel de Morlet, their seventy-year-old maternal grandfather.

Charles was a laughing, affectionate child with a lively imagination and a will of his own. The kindly old colonel, despite a lifetime in the army, proved a poor disciplinarian. Young Charles soon discovered that a well-orchestrated tantrum could get him anything. "When he cries he reminds me of my daughter," sighed the grandfather, surrendering without a fight. Not only was Charles self-willed, he was also greedy. At parties he would swoop on the cakes before the other children had a chance, and gobble up the whole plateful.

The wayward young glutton was eleven when his cousin, Marie Moitessier, first took him under her wing. Marie was eight years older, a beautiful young woman with a profound spiritual life and a special devotion to the Sacred Heart. On a long holiday at her family's summer home, Marie took her orphan cousin for long walks, just as his father had done before tuberculosis finally robbed him of his strength. Marie's deep piety reminded Charles of the mother whom he had lost so soon after his father: the mother, herself so devout, who had taught him his prayers.

The accord begun that summer never broke or faltered; it endured until Charles's death. Undoubtedly it was one of the great spiritual friendships of all time. Yet we know maddeningly little about it, because Marie's letters to Charles have not survived, and we only have fragments of his to her.

When Charles, at high school age, began to lose his faith, Marie did not lecture or badger him; nor did she when, at a Jesuit boarding school, his amorous exploits with shop girls got him into trouble. At age seventeen he was, by his own account, "all egoism, vanity, impiety, evil-doing." Yet Marie, now the Vicomtesse de Bondy, remained as cheerful and affectionate as ever.

Charles needed all her affection, for he was desperately unhappy at school. The regime was strict and the work hard; the day began at 4:40 a.m. Charles, who was neither lazy nor stupid, virtually went on strike, hoping to be expelled. Meanwhile, he consoled himself with mountains of cakes and put on weight alarmingly. In March 1876, the Jesuits gave in. Charles was asked to leave.

At the military academy of Saint Cyr he worked hard at first, but his grandfather's death in February 1879 seems to have thrown him off-balance, and his studies suffered badly. However, he finished with the rank of sub-lieutenant and went on to the cavalry school at Saumur. There, on his twentieth birthday, he inherited a fortune from his grandfather.

His extravagance made him the talk of the town. Every night he gorged himself at a fashionable restaurant. He threw wild parties for his friends. He patronized the best hairdresser, the best bootmaker, and the best tailor. When he entertained, he hired all the cabs in town for the whole evening, instructing them to drive around until they were needed.

Of course, there were many women. "I rent by the day, not by the month," he told one mistress with brutal honesty.

He began to play strange pranks. On one occasion he got himself arrested when he entered a restaurant wearing an obviously false beard and the manager took him for a bandit.

Another escapade now seems highly significant. One morning he disappeared from the school. As days passed without any trace of him, alarm grew. Police mounted a search. After nearly a month, he was discovered wandering through the countryside in a beggar's rags.

"I got fed up with comfort and luxury," he explained. "I wanted to feel for myself what it was to be poor."

Graduating from Saumur eighty-seventh in a class of eighty-seven, Charles found himself at Pont-à-Mousson, near Nancy. There he set up house with a lady known as Mimi.

Now the army had no objection to his keeping a mistress, but when the regiment was posted to Algeria and Charles tried to pass off Mimi as the Vicomtesse de Foucauld, authority came down with a firm hand. Charles received an ultimatum: Mimi must go. Charles was defiant: The lady, he pointed out, was not subject to military discipline. The case was referred to Paris. Charles was removed from active service.

It was not long before he realized his mistake, for now Africa was in his blood. Living with Mimi beside Lake Geneva, he continued to study Arabic and African history. The more he studied, the more unhappy and restless he became. Finally, bidding Mimi a fond farewell, he asked to be reinstated in the army.

Gone now was the greedy, indolent playboy. For eight months the young officer fought bravely and skillfully against rebels in South Oran. When the campaign was over, however, he found that he could not face the boredom of a garrison town.

When he was refused a place in an army expedition to the Niger, his stubborn streak emerged once more, though this time to excellent effect. He resigned his commission and resolved to satisfy an ambition that had been growing inside him. He would explore Morocco, a vast territory that was then little-known and whose relations with France were uneasy.

To travel under his own name would be to invite almost certain death, for a Christian European would inevitably be suspected of spying. He would have to adopt a disguise — but what disguise? He could not hope to pass himself off as a Muslim. Only one alternative remained: He would play the part of a Jew. As a Jew he would be tolerated and, he hoped, ignored; for Jews were despised by their Muslim neighbors, and so long as they did not get in the way, they generally went unnoticed.

Dressed in the robes of an Oriental rabbi and speaking bad French, Charles set out from Algiers on the first leg of his highly dangerous mission. His companion and guide was one Mardochée, a genuine rabbi who knew his way around but who was given to endless complaints and sudden fits of weeping. He and Charles quarreled frequently and fiercely.

Officially Charles was Rabbi Joseph Aliman, a Russian-born man of God who also practiced medicine. He did indeed carry a medicine chest, but he also carried a box loaded with barometers, sextants, maps, and other instruments. For Charles was not simply out for adventure; he wanted to make a name for himself as a scientific explorer.

In this he succeeded spectacularly. His accurately drawn maps, the first the West had seen, earned him the gold medal of the Paris Geographical Society. Later his book *Reconnaisance au Maroc* won him applause all over Europe — and what an exciting story it told!

Several times during his journey through the forbidden land, Charles had been suspect. No fewer than four times he was forced to admit his true identity. Each time his confidant proved trustworthy. One Arab sheik, believing Charles a French spy, nevertheless gave him VIP treatment. He thought it would stand him in good stead if France invaded Morocco.

Mostly, however, his disguise was successful. Once, as he sat in a dusty square eating bread and olives, a party of French officers rode by. Some of them Charles actually knew. "Look at that little Jew eating olives," said one, pointing at him. "He looks just like a monkey."

Where possible the travelers lodged with Jewish families or spent the night in a synagogue. Traveling across deserts, he and his companion depended on Arab guides, who extorted money with thinly veiled threats. On one occasion they were actually seized and robbed, and Charles had to listen while, for two days, his captors argued about whether or not to cut his throat.

Soon after his return to Algeria, Charles was in the home of Commandant Titre, a distinguished French geographer, when a girl walked into the room. She was twenty-three, dark, vivacious, and very beautiful. Then and there Charles fell in love with her — or at least, so he thought. Soon they were engaged.

Charles's fiancée was a deeply religious girl who had sacrificed a large inheritance from her Protestant grandmother in order to become a Catholic. "When we are married," Charles told her, "you will be perfectly free to practice your religion, but you must not expect me to join you. I cannot believe."

In fact the engagement was short-lived. Charles's relatives objected that the young lady was socially inferior: Her name lacked the *particule* of the aristocracy. (In later life, Charles dropped the "de" from his own name.) Marie de Bondy also played a part in breaking up the relationship, though we may be sure that her motives were very different. "I needed to be saved from marriage," he wrote later, "and you saved me."

Is it likely that a man as strong-willed as Charles would have let Marie dissuade him from marriage if he had really been determined to go ahead? For now he was a very mature person indeed — as his fiancée herself testified when, many years later, she gave evidence to the postulator of his cause.

"At twenty-five there was certainly nothing of the child left in him," she declared. "He returned from Morocco a serious man, more serious than many other men at forty-five. He knew life and, humanly speaking, he had become wise."

Clearly Charles broke off the engagement because of his own inner misgivings, though what they were he never disclosed. Was he, though still an agnostic, feeling the first stirrings of his true vocation? For not only had his Moroccan adventures made him wise, they had given him something greater still: a growing sense of the spiritual. During these dangerous wanderings, he had watched with new eyes as the Muslims, so utterly devoted to their religion, dropped all their activities to pray five times a day.

"Islam shook me deeply," he wrote long afterward. "Seeing such faith, seeing people living in the continual presence of God, I came to glimpse something worthy and more real than worldly occupations." He had, moreover, lived as a Jew among Jews, and he marveled at their fidelity to the faith of Moses in the teeth of the contempt that he, in his rabbi's robes, had to share. When, on their Sabbath, they refused to travel or to perform any other task, Charles was exasperated. But he was also deeply impressed.

Whatever explanation he gave to his fiancée, she was brokenhearted at losing him. Many years later, in 1913, they met once more in the streets of Algiers. She was now a married woman, he a priest. She told him that she was no longer a Catholic. Knowing that he was the cause, he prayed for her. In time, she came back to the Church.

She never forgot Charles, never got over the pain of losing him. "He would have made a perfect husband," she told the postulator, "and I have pined for him all my life, and I loved him and will love him until my dying day."

She uttered those words on her sixty-fifth birthday. Charles had been dead for ten years.

His engagement broken, Charles returned to France. He took an apartment in Paris on the Rue de Miromesnil, near the Church of Saint Augustin. There he worked on his book, taking occasional walks for exercise. When Marie de Bondy was in Paris, he saw her often. The more he saw of her, the more he began to ask himself: "If she, who is so intelligent, can also be so devout, is religion, after all, the foolishness I had imagined it to be?"

More and more frequently his walks led him to Saint Augustin or to one of the other churches of the capital. Soon he was murmuring: "O God, if you really do exist, please let me know it."

He was bound to meet the Abbé Huvelin, for not only was the priest a neighbor, he was also Marie's spiritual director, and it was Marie who brought them together. This remarkable priest, a brilliant historian and classical scholar, had turned down a college professorship in order to take an unpaid post at Saint Augustin. Day by day he sat in his room, a cat on his knees, racked by pain and illness, yet receiving the rich and the famous, the poor and the downtrodden, with equal kindness and equal attention to their needs.

He had, in a remarkable degree, the gift of looking straight into a soul and knowing in a flash what medicine to prescribe. Hence his bold approach when Charles appeared in his confessional that October morning — and what a stroke of genius it proved to be! From now on the Abbé Huvelin would guide Charles as he had guided so many others.

With Marie he began to go often to Benediction. Soon he had a deep devotion to the Blessed Sacrament.

Under the Abbé Huvelin's influence, Charles made a pilgrimage to the Holy Land, arriving in December when Jerusalem was covered in snow. The conviction grew within him that he must dedicate his life to God. Earlier, with Marie and her family, he had visited the Trappist Abbey of Fontgombaut and had been deeply impressed to see that a lay brother wore a ragged habit. Long ago, at Saumur, poverty had suddenly seemed attractive to him — so attractive that he had run away to taste it. Now it began to present itself as an ideal.

"It was you who brought me to the Trappists," Charles wrote later to Marie, but his decision to join the order was not made in haste. It was not until December 1889 that he finally made up his mind. On January 15, 1890, at seven in the evening, he left Paris for the Abbey of Notre Dame-des-Neiges in the Ardeche.

Earlier in the day he said goodbye to the Abbé Huvelin, who was ill. The remaining hours were spent mostly with Marie. When he left for the station, he was crying.

Were they in love, these two, perhaps without admitting it even to themselves? It is tempting to believe that they were. The thought was voiced even in the first days of Charles's conversion, when someone unkindly called Marie's husband "a spiritual cuckold." But Olivier de Bondy never saw himself in that light. He and Charles were always good friends.

What is clear is that Marie replaced, and continued to replace, the mother whom he had lost so early in life. On their journey to Fontgombault, some people actually mistook her for his mother. "I cannot tell you how much happiness that mistake brought me," he wrote later. Whether Marie was equally pleased, we are not told. She was, after all, only eight years his senior.

Charles was an exemplary Trappist. Even in that company of holy men, he stood out. He performed the meanest tasks cheerfully and willingly. He undertook penances more severe than those demanded by the Rule. Even on Easter Sunday, the glutton of Saumur refused to take more than bread and water. He slept for only two hours a night.

And yet he did not stay. First at Notre Dame-des-Neiges, then at an even poorer monastery at Cheikle, in Syria, the conviction grew in him that he was not a Trappist at heart. He found the Rule narrow and constricting. He preferred long hours of mental prayer to the chanting of the office in choir, and he felt irritated at being constantly required to change his tasks.

Most of all, incredible though it may seem, he thought the Trappists lived too well. He objected to the distinction between choir and lay brothers, and he was scandalized that the monastery employed outside labor. Syria did nothing to change his mind. He compared the Trappist life with that of the neighboring peasants and decided that, poor as they were, the monks had a better deal. This came home to him one night as he sat at the bedside of a dying workman. The monastery might be a collection of huts, the meals might be sparse, but at least the monks knew where the next one was coming from. They did not share the anxiety, the total insecurity, of true poverty.

By the time he was released from his vows, Charles had been sent to Rome to further his studies of theology. His superiors, despite his unwillingness, wanted him to be ordained.

The Trappists were sorry to see him go, though some of them recognized that his was a very special sort of sanctity, not one that could be contained by any Rule. "How lucky you are to have been given this unique vocation!" the father-general told him before he left.

The next three years were spent in the Holy Land, at Nazareth and Jerusalem. In each place he lived beside the Poor Clares' convent, doing odd jobs for the nuns. At Nazareth he often painted pictures that the nuns were able to sell.

He had arrived in Palestine with a costume that, he fondly imagined, resembled that of the local peasants. It provoked much merriment among the Arab urchins, who threw stones at him whenever he appeared. In return he gave them nuts and sweets, offering their scorn joyfully to our Lord.

One of Charles's great-uncles, a priest, had been killed in the French Revolution. As a child Charles had sometimes dreamed of dying for the faith. Now he wrote a strange, partly prophetic meditation. "Think that you ought to die a martyr, stripped of everything, stretched naked on the ground and unrecognizable, covered with wounds and blood, killed violently and painfully — desire that it be today."

Meanwhile he dreamed of founding a new kind of religious order, where new communities would live together in Gospel simplicity, offering help and hospitality to all who needed it.

When the Mount of the Beatitudes came onto the market, Charles tried to buy it as a home for his new order. But the deal came to nothing; a swindling middleman robbed him of the cash.

For the present, although the nuns called him Brother Charles, his order consisted solely of himself. Naturally this hermit handyman, with his obvious breeding and his perfect manners, aroused much curiosity. Soon gossip began to circulate.

"Monsieur, they say you are a vicomte," a Salesian lay brother observed one day.

"I used to be a soldier," replied Charles, remaining noncommittal about the color of his blood.

That he was still a soldier he demonstrated one evening in Jerusalem, when three Italian roughnecks arrived at the convent and demanded a meal that the desperately poor sisters were not able to provide. They were starting to get nasty when Charles arrived on the scene in best U.S. cavalry style.

"Come on," he said curtly. "Out!"

The men hesitated. Charles did not. Seizing the biggest, he flung him through the gate and his two companions after him.

"I'm sorry," he told the astonished nuns. "That wasn't very edifying."

He had gone to the Jerusalem convent because the superior, who had the Nazareth convent in her jurisdiction, wanted to see this Brother Charles for herself. She half-suspected that he might be a phony, but once she had met him she swiftly decided that here was no pious layabout, sponging on the nuns, but a man of very unusual qualities indeed.

In fact she was to play a decisive role in his life, for it was she, even more than Marie or the Abbé Huvelin himself, who prompted and encouraged Charles in his decision to become a priest.

"I quite understand your desire to keep the lowest place," she told him. "I see why you draw back from the honor which the priesthood commands. Nevertheless, it is as a priest that you must use the gifts which God has given to you. Quite clearly, this is your vocation — and you have, after all, completed most of your studies."

In August 1900 he sailed for France. Ten months later, on June 1, 1901, he was ordained.

His first thought was to return to the Holy Land, where he had lived so happily for three years. But the Holy Land was full of priests. Surely the life of Nazareth could be lived anywhere?

In Morocco, a country as large as France, there was not a single priest; in the whole of the Sahara, seven times larger, only a handful of missionaries. It had been through the example of Muslims and Jews that Charles's thoughts had been turned back to God. Now, he decided, he would spend the rest of his life among non-Christians, sharing their poverty and preaching the Gospel by living it.

"I want everyone here, Christian, Muslim, Jew, pagan, to look on me as a brother, a universal brother," he wrote Marie soon after his arrival. "Here" was Beni Abbès, an oasis in Northern Algeria near the border with Morocco.

Helped by soldiers from the nearby garrison, he built his hermitage of mud bricks and palm trunks: a group of low, reddish-brown buildings set around a courtyard, with cells for the brothers who never came.

"Already they are calling this house the 'fraternity' — *khousa* in Arabic — and I am delighted," he wrote. "They realize that the poor have a brother here — not only the poor, though, all men."

Being a brother to all proved a wearying business, Charles quickly found. From early morning onward, a procession of soldiers, slaves, travelers, and peasants came and went. Everyone sought the help of this Christian *marabout*, this strange holy man with his gentle, ascetic face and the red heart and cross on his Arab-style robe. For the soldiers he would say Mass whenever they needed it, at midnight or at four in the morning. He had expected to live a life of prayer and contemplation, but here he was as busy as any city pastor. Yet pray he did, constantly.

Charles was outraged that the French colonial rulers allowed slavery to flourish without restraint. All over Algeria, in the name of liberty, equality, and fraternity, men and women went shackled and children were stolen from their parents to be sold in slave markets. Charles thought that the Church should cry out against such cruelty, as Pope Leo XIII already had done in Rome. But the French bishops, unwilling to provoke an anticlerical government, preferred diplomatic whispers.

Whispers were not Charles's style. "One of the things we absolutely owe to our Lord," he declared, "is never to be afraid." For him Jesus was "Master of the Impossible."

Whenever slaves sought his help he never turned them away, though housing them was a major problem. Some he managed to free by buying them with money from his family. He also cared for slaves who, too old to work, had been turned loose without means of support.

Though a mystic, living in close union with God, Charles remained a man among men. Invited to dine in the officers' mess, he did not turn a hair when some Montmartre songs were played on the gramophone. Marshal Lyavtey, an old friend of Charles, was the guest of honor. "I said to myself, 'He'll go out now,'" the marshal recalled later, "but he didn't. He was actually laughing!"

Next day the marshal and some of his brother officers attended Mass in the hermitage. He described the experience with soldierly bluntness.

"What a hovel! The chapel a miserable corridor, with columns covered with reeds! A plank for an altar! Tin-plate candlesticks and the only decoration a picture of Christ on calico! And our feet in the sand. I certainly never heard Mass in the way Father de Foucauld said his. I thought I was in the Egypt of the Desert Fathers. For me it will always be one of the great experiences of my life."

The old warrior had understood instinctively why Charles lived as he did. Not everyone was so perceptive. More than once, Charles had to endure the taunts of godless soldiers and officials.

In 1905 another army friend, General Laperrine, asked Charles to move to southern Algeria to work among the Tuareg of the Hoggar region. The Tuareg were not Arabs but Berbers, a fair-skinned people with a language of their own, descended from Phoenicians.

Charles hesitated long, but decided to go after he had consulted the Abbé Huvelin. He knew the dangers, for many

Frenchmen had been killed by Tuareg warriors, among them one of his friends from Saint Cyr and Saumur. If he felt any fear, he quelled it at once. In Charles's book, fear was a sure sign of a duty to be done.

Despite their proud history and dignified bearing, the Tuareg were miserably poor, racked by disease and apt to strangle unwanted children at birth. Some of their other habits, though less sinister, were highly uncongenial. Their womenfolk never washed because they thought it harmed their health. Charles decided that, as soon as they became available, Frenchwomen would teach their Tuareg sisters the use of soap and water.

His new hermitage was at Tamanrasset, an oasis close to the Hoggar mountains. Here, as before, he ministered to all who came. Yet he also contrived to spend long hours before the Blessed Sacrament in his tiny chapel.

A vivid picture of life with Charles comes from Brother Michael, the only novice whom he ever recruited. He was a Breton fisherman's son, who had first been a student with the White Fathers, then a soldier.

After waking Michael at dawn, Charles rang a bell summoning him to chapel. As they both slept fully dressed, it did not take long to get there. Devotions began with a long prayer in French and Latin, then there was exposition of the Blessed Sacrament, Mass, and silent prayer. Charles himself never ate before eleven o'clock, but at seven he sent Michael out to breakfast on coffee and cake.

Work began at nine. Charles shut himself in the tiny sacristy, where he dealt with his huge correspondence and worked on his Tuareg-French dictionary. This unique work took ten years to complete and would have given Charles a lasting reputation as a scholar even if he had no other claim to fame. While Charles was writing, Michael read, crushed dates, ground flour between two stones, and baked bread.

Before the main meal, at eleven, there was a New Testament reading. They ate sitting on mats beside the saucepan, fishing out the food with a spoon. The main dish was always boiled rice, sometimes mixed with condensed milk and sometimes with carrots or turnips. Dessert, which Michael quite enjoyed, was a sort of jam made from crushed dates, flour and water. Supper was much the same, but there was one course only.

Determined to keep his needs to a minimum, Charles wrote his letters on the backs of old envelopes, which he slit and opened out for the purpose. His "desk" was a packing case; through constantly leaning over it, he eventually developed a slight stoop.

When Michael finally decided that the desert was not for him, Charles was not altogether sorry. He thought the young man somewhat lacking in intelligence, which may or may not have been true. It is possible that Charles was sometimes impatient with lesser men, and Michael himself noted that he could be irritable when things did not go as he wished.

So Michael went off to the Carthusians, where he at last found his vocation, and Charles waited in vain for someone to take his place. One of the saddest entries in his diary is for Christmas Day 1907: "No Mass, for I am alone." Permission to celebrate without server or congregation had not yet arrived from Rome.

Yet solitude was an essential element in his vocation. "One must cross the desert and live there to receive God's grace," he wrote. "It is there that one can drive away from oneself everything that is not God."

It was not a new discovery, of course. Saint Anthony of Egypt and the first monks sought God in the wilderness centuries before. Today the brothers and sisters who follow in Charles's footsteps make a retreat alone, in a desert environment, as part of their training.

It is easy to imagine that for such chosen souls as Charles, serving God is somehow easier than for the rest of us; that despite all the hardships, Charles somehow passed all his days in a happy haze. In fact, despite that dramatic start in the Abbé Huvelin's confessional, Charles's conversion was a long, painful, step-by-step process.

Once, in the desert, an officer reproached him for fasting to excess.

"My friend," replied Charles, "when you want to write on a blackboard, you must first wipe off what is written there. I have, I assure you, a great deal to wipe off my board!"

He could and did feel periods of aridity, when God seemed far away. Perhaps the ex-agnostic was remembering these when he wrote about the virtue of faith:

"It is nearly always faith which our Lord praises and rewards. Sometimes he praises love, sometimes humility, but this is rare . . . Faith, though not the supreme virtue — charity holds that place — is nevertheless the most important because it is the basis of all the others, charity included. Also it is the rarest . . . Real faith, faith which inspires all one's actions, faith in the supernatural which strips the world of its mask and reveals God in everything, which makes meaningless the words 'impossible,' 'anxiety,' 'danger,' and 'fear' . . . how rare that is!"

When war came in 1914, members of the fanatical Senussi sect tried to persuade the Tuareg to rebel against the French. The Tuareg, however, remained loyal to France, chiefly because they were loyal to their Christian *marabout*.

On December 1, 1916, Charles had bolted himself inside the *bordj*, the small, fort-like building where he lived at Taman-rasset. Hearing a loud knocking and a familiar voice calling his name, he unbolted the door and opened it.

At once he was seized by a group of Senussi, bound, and forced to squat in front of the building. A Judas had betrayed him; the voice he heard belonged to a half-caste Tuareg to whom he had been kind. "It is God's will," he murmured, as the Senussi, leaving a fifteen-year-old boy to guard him, ransacked the *bordj*.

Probably they did not intend to kill him, but at that moment two Arab soldiers from the nearby garrison galloped toward them, evidently intending to visit the *marabout*. In an effort to warn them, Charles made a swift gesture. The boy, armed with a loaded rifle, panicked and fired. Brother Charles of Jesus, Vicomte de Foucauld, fell dead with a bullet through his brain.

"When you set out to do something," he wrote once, "you had better not come back without having done it."

Poignant words, you may think, from the missionary who scarcely made a single convert; from the founder who died without a single follower.

But Charles was not a missionary in the ordinary sense. He did not set out to make converts directly, but to show the Muslims, already so devout, the life of Christ in living reality.

And the order, which he failed so dismally to establish? "Where I sow, others will reap," he prophesied. Today no fewer than five religious congregations, three of women and two of men, carry on his work; not only in the deserts of Africa, but in the downtown deserts of Chicago and Washington, London and Leeds. Everywhere they share the life of the poor, taking jobs alongside them, identifying with them in a totally new form of religious life. In a Venezuelan jungle, on a Hong Kong junk, tending sheep in Provence, running a dispensary in Benares, in factories, hospitals — even in prisons — these humble, heroic men and women follow in Charles's footsteps. They are the harvest that he sowed when, on that December night in 1916, his blood ran out onto the sand.

10

"CHRIST STREAMED OUT
UPON ME"

Saint Edith Stein

As soon as the two officials stated their business, the prioress knew something sinister was happening.

"We have come to supervise the voting by the nuns," they announced.

"That will not be necessary," the prioress told them. "Although ours is an enclosed order, the sisters are always allowed out to vote in the normal way."

One of the men, evidently the senior, snapped back: "The voting will take place here in the convent — immediately."

Long years as a Carmelite helped the prioress to retain her calm. It was useless to argue with these men, she knew that. They were Nazis, and they had their orders.

When each nun had recorded her vote, the senior official consulted a list.

"Two persons have not voted," he declared. "Anna Fitzeck is missing."

"She does not have a vote — she is mentally handicapped," the prioress explained.

The junior official made a note. The prioress knew only too well what was coming next.

"And Dr. Edith Stein? Where is she?"

The prioress tried even harder not to betray her anxiety. "Sister Mary Benedicta is not entitled to vote."

"Why not?"

"She is not Aryan."

Both men stared at her for a moment. When the senior spoke, his voice was hard.

"Write that down," he ordered. "Dr. Edith Stein, otherwise known as Sister Mary Benedicta — non-Aryan."

With that the two men departed. In the election, to nobody's surprise, the Nazis won a landmark victory.

She could no longer stay in the Cologne Carmel — Edith knew that at once. The presence of a Jewish nun in a German convent would soon bring harassment, and perhaps worse, on the whole community.

But Holland was safe, for this was still 1938, and the Carmel at Echt offered her a loving welcome. So to Echt she went, driven by a kindly doctor friend.

As they neared the Dutch border, he stopped at a wayside shrine of Our Lady of Peace. There Edith knelt and prayed for Germany, the country of her birth; the country that, though she did not know it then, she was leaving for the last time.

It had been a long, winding road that had brought her from a devoutly Orthodox Jewish home, via years of atheism, at last to the Catholic Church and to Carmel. Perhaps she looked back over that road, this beautiful, dark-eyed woman of forty-seven, as the car sped through the flat Dutch countryside.

Edith Stein was born in Breslau on October 12, 1891. Her father, a timber merchant, died when she was a baby, and upon her mother fell the double responsibility of running the business and caring for a growing family of seven. Fortunately she was a tough, energetic woman; qualities that Edith, her youngest child, inherited in full.

One of Edith's brothers, Paul, had a great love of literature, and he would often talk to Edith about Goethe, Schiller, and Heine as he carried her around in his arms. By the time she was four, little Jitschell — as her family called her — could reel off the salient details about all the major German poets.

There was friction when she went to kindergarten — no place for a four-year-old intellectual. Having swiftly exhausted the teacher, Edith was returned home to await her sixth birthday, when she could go to a proper school and do proper lessons.

During her later schooldays she got her first taste of anti-Semitism, when she was passed over for a prize everyone knew she had won. Ironically, she had by this time abandoned her Jewish faith, at least inwardly. She still went to synagogue, but only to please her mother. At thirteen, Edith no longer believed in God.

Despite her Jewish birth, Edith admired the Prussian character; throughout her own life she practiced its iron self-discipline. At school she was invariably top of the class. Yet she did not suffer the unpopularity that sometimes goes with that position, for she had a warm and affectionate nature beneath her outward reserve, and her flashes of humor were all the more delightful for being unexpected. Furthermore she was not *quite* perfect; in arithmetic lessons her brilliance sometimes dimmed, and when that happened she was not above copying the answers from her friend Katharina.

Edith did not study to win prizes or to outshine her classmates, but because she loved knowledge for its own sake. In one of her school essays she wrote: "A translator must be like a pane of glass, letting all the light shine through while itself remaining invisible."

The teenager had produced an epigram worthy of a classical author, and although she did not do that every day, she had a maturity of judgment far beyond her years. Small wonder that when she left, the principal made a pun on her surname: "Strike the stone (*stein*) and wisdom will spring forth."

At the University of Breslau she enrolled as a student of German language and literature, but philosophy was a compulsory subject and she soon realized that this was where her heart lay. In particular, she was captivated by the new school of thought known as phenomenology, whose leading exponent, Edmund Husserl, was then teaching at the University of Göttingen.

So hooked on Husserl was she that her friends twitted her about it. At a New Year's party they made up a song that contained the following immortal lines:

> *Other maidens dream of kisses*
> *Husserl is what Edith wishes.*

(In German the philosopher's name is made to rhyme with *busserl*, a dialect word meaning "kisses.")

After two years at Breslau, Edith's dream came true. With a girlfriend she moved to Göttingen to study under the great man.

Though she would have been astonished had anyone told her so, Edith had taken her first step toward her eventual conversion to the Catholic Church. Phenomenology asserts that there is a real and objective world that can be known by the human mind: a view more in tune with traditional Catholic philosophy than other modern schools of thought. (Pope John Paul II, himself a former professor of philosophy, is an expert on Husserl and his work.)

Husserl sometimes joked that he ought to be canonized, as so many of his pupils became Catholics (though born a Jew, he was now a Lutheran). We can only guess what he might have said had he known that one of his pupils would become not only a Catholic, but a canonized saint.

Before meeting her idol, Edith had to present herself to his assistant, Max Reinach. Soon she was a firm friend of the kindly young philosopher and the pretty wife whom he had recently married.

At her first, awestruck encounter with Husserl, Edith told him that she had read the whole of his masterwork *Logical*

Investigations, including the difficult second volume. "You have?" Husserl smiled, eyes twinkling. "That really is heroic."

Among the students at his seminars, Edith's razor-sharp mind soon showed its quality. So it was not really surprising that in 1916, when he became professor of philosophy at Freiburg, Husserl invited her to go with him as his assistant.

A short time before, such an offer would have been beyond her wildest hopes. She ought to have been happy — but somehow she was not. She had now spent years in the study of philosophy. She was at the right hand of the teacher she admired above all. And yet . . . her quest for truth remained unsatisfied.

As she worked on Husserl's papers, producing order from piles of rough shorthand notes, the conviction grew within her that neither phenomenology nor any other philosophical system could answer her ultimate need. Could religion help her? She could never return to the Jewish faith of her childhood, of that she was sure. But what of Christianity?

During her first year at university she had been required to study the Lord's Prayer in the Old High German language, and this careful, step-by-step analysis had made a deep impression on her. Now she began to reflect on the prayer once again.

Among Husserl's converts was Max Scheler, a Jew like herself; a brilliant but erratic character who twice abandoned his Catholic faith, the second time never to return to it. When Edith knew him he was between apostasies and at his most fervent. Whatever his faults, he helped her on the journey she had begun.

In 1917 Adolf Reinach was killed while fighting for Germany. He, too, had been a Jew, but both he and his wife had, like Husserl, been baptized as Lutherans. Edith, herself grief-stricken, went to see the young widow, dreading that she would find her distraught.

To Edith's surprise, Anna Reinach was completely calm; her Christian faith had given her courage to bear her loss. At this time she was still a Protestant, though subsequently she was received into the Catholic Church.

Of her visit to Anna, Edith wrote later: "It was then that I first came face-to-face with the cross and the divine strength which it gave to those who bear it... Christ streamed out upon me."

Even so, Edith did not become a Catholic, not yet. It was not in her nature to rush into things.

In 1921 she spent a holiday with friends who ran a farm at Bergzabern. Among their books she found Saint Teresa of Ávila's autobiography. Quite literally she could not put it down — and she did not, until she had finished the last page. When she did finally close it, in the small hours of the morning, she knew that she must become a Catholic.

Baptized on New Year's Day 1922, she went home to Breslau to break the news. For the first time in her life, she saw her mother cry.

To comfort her, Edith went several times with her to the synagogue. To Frau Stein's great astonishment her daughter followed the service closely, reading the psalms from a Catholic breviary. In this way Edith tried to show her mother that her baptism was no act of treachery — that indeed she had recovered the faith of her childhood in all its glorious fulfillment.

With her conversion to Catholicism came the firm conviction that she must also follow Saint Teresa by becoming a Carmelite nun. Yet she could not bring herself to enter at once. Her mother, already shattered by her conversion, might not survive the loss of her daughter behind convent walls.

The next eight years she spent teaching at a girls' school run by the Dominican nuns at Speyer, a medieval city beside the Rhine. There she spent long hours in prayer, reciting the Divine Office each day. Asked to teach Latin to the younger sisters, she was soon giving spiritual conferences as well. Although

Edith was a laywoman and a recent convert, the nuns were quick to recognize her very real holiness.

She was, predictably, a strict and demanding teacher. When a girl said that she could not write an essay because she had injured her right hand, Edith told her to do it with her left. On another occasion the same girl handed in a currant bun of an essay, stuffed with quotations. She expected a good mark, but it came back inscribed: "The use of quotations proves that *other* people are clever."

Yet her door was always open to anyone with a problem, and she proved the wisest of counselors to nuns and students alike. She was never flippant or sarcastic, but she knew how to laugh. German schoolteachers of that era often thought it their duty to be formidable. Edith's pupils, meeting her outside the classroom, were at first surprised and then delighted by her easy, friendly manner.

When the girls studied *Hamlet* in school, Edith won permission for them to see the play performed in the professional theater — an unheard-of concession. Throughout her life she was an ardent campaigner for women's education; even as a Carmelite she did not hide her opinion that the Church still had much to do in this area. She considered herself a feminist, although not everyone would call her so today, for she always insisted women's helping, serving role was essential to their nature.

During her eight years at Speyer, Edith worked on German translations of Newman and Saint Thomas Aquinas. She kept abreast of philosophical thought and grew in her love of prayer. But there was another side to her life. Often she could be seen slipping quietly into town with a parcel under her arm — a present for some poor family or for someone down on his luck.

Despite her beauty and her affectionate personality, Edith seems never to have had any romantic attachments, either before or after she became a Catholic. "Academic life imposes its own obligations," she confided to a friend. "I have always lived like a nun."

She finally entered Carmel in 1934, after a period as a college lecturer in Munster. As she feared, her mother took the parting very badly, though she bravely tried not to blame Christ for taking away her daughter. "I won't say anything against him," she cried in her distress. "He may have been a very good man. But why did he make himself God?"

Frau Stein was now eighty-four years old, and to leave her almost tore Edith's heart out. Yet even as she said goodbye, she knew even more certainly that she was doing what was right.

"Is she a good with the needle?" one of the Cologne sisters asked anxiously when she learned that Dr. Edith Stein was to enter as a postulant. In the convent, for the first time in her life, the philosopher found herself working hard with mop and duster, and it has to be said that she did not do very well at it. Nevertheless she tried, even the most exacting of the sisters had to admit that, as they watched her rubbing her way gamely along the corridors.

Before she entered the convent, Edith had sometimes been guilty of looking askance at those who did not come up to her own high standards of duty and self-discipline. In particular, she could not understand how anyone could grow tired while at prayer. One day, soon after entering, she said as much.

The other nuns were living the Carmelite rule in all its strictness, and they understood very well how tiring it could be. But they made no comment; they just waited. Then came the day when Edith, now herself a professed Carmelite, fell asleep at her prayers. She was never censorious again.

As she grew into her new life, she became more relaxed. Saint Teresa of Ávila had laughed loud and often, and so did Edith, sometimes until the tears ran down her cheeks.

Her superiors, not wishing her talents to lie buried, encouraged her to write. She produced a study of Husserl's philosophy in relation to that of Saint Thomas Aquinas, and much other work besides.

Yet over these happy, fruitful years lay the shadow of the swastika — a shadow that for her became a reality when the two Nazi officials knocked at the door of the Cologne Carmel on that election day in 1938.

When she fled to Holland, it was for the sake of her sisters. It was not in her nature to seek safety for herself, nor did she desire it.

Edith, who had been born on the Jewish Day of Atonement, now offered her own life as a sacrifice for peace, praying that a new world war might be avoided. She wrote out her wish to her new prioress in the Carmel at Echt. The note, still preserved, is dated March 26, 1939 — Passion Sunday.

When war broke out and the Nazis invaded Holland, her sacrifice was accepted. Her superiors had arranged that she should go to a Carmel in Switzerland with her sister Rosa, who had come to live at the convent. As the formalities for her exit visa were being completed, the Dutch bishops published a pastoral letter protesting the Nazis' ill-treatment of the Jews. The invaders retaliated swiftly. Among their victims were Edith and Rosa Stein.

When the SS guards came for them, Edith turned and said: "Pray, sisters, pray." To Rosa she said: "Come, we are going for our people."

Taken to a camp at Westerbork, they were treated roughly and thrust into a hut where they spent the day without food. Among their fellow prisoners were mothers with babies and young children, some of them so afraid that they could not look after their children properly. A Jew who escaped told later of a Carmelite nun who moved serenely from group to group, comforting the mothers and tending the little ones.

As a train packed with Jewish prisoners moved through Germany, it stopped at Schifferstadt. Standing on the station platform was a woman who had been a pupil of Edith at the Dominican school at Speyer. Suddenly hearing someone call her by her maiden name, the woman looked up and saw Edith at one of the train's windows. "Give my love to the sisters at Saint Magdalena," she said. "I am going toward the East."

Two days later, on August 9, 1942, Edith Stein died with her sister in the gas chamber at Auschwitz. She was beatified on May 1, 1987, and canonized on October 11, 1998.

11

"MY REIGN WILL BE
A SHORT ONE"

Pope John Paul I

On September 29, 1978, a stunned world awoke to the news that Pope John Paul I had died suddenly during the night, barely a month after ascending to the papal throne. Before his election, on August 26, Cardinal Albino Luciani was little known outside Italy. Yet during his brief reign, he conquered the world with his simple, unfeigned warmth. The media quickly dubbed him "the smiling pope."

The election of the diminutive Cardinal Luciani came as a surprise to almost everyone outside the Sacred College. Yet it happened with remarkable speed, on the first day of the conclave. In Saint Peter's Square, a huge crowd fixed its eyes on the tiny chimney connected to the stove in which the cardinals' ballots were burned. If no candidate had been elected, damp straw would be added to the papers and the resulting smoke would be black. White smoke would signal a new pope.

After the first three ballots, the smoke had been unmistakably black. After the fourth, it emerged an ambiguous gray color. Bewildered watchers asked each other whether there had been an election or another hung vote.

They did not have to wait long for an answer. Above the great central door of Saint Peter's, the senior cardinal deacon, Cardinal Felici, appeared on the balcony to make the time-honored Latin proclamation: "*Nuntio vobis gaudium magnum. Habemus Papam!*" — "I announce to you a great joy. We have a pope!" Moments later the new pope gave the world its first glimpse of the smile that was to become his trademark — a slightly impish smile, eyes twinkling behind glasses and a peak of graying hair pushing from beneath the white skullcap.

As always before a papal election, the media had named several cardinals as *papabile* — likely candidates for the throne of Peter. Few mentioned the name of Albino Luciani, the patriarch of Venice, and those who did viewed him merely as an outsider. Unlike previous popes, he had served neither in the curia nor as a papal diplomat. So how did the conclave come to elect him so quickly?

One answer came from Britain's Cardinal Basil Hume. For him, Luciani was "God's candidate." He declared: "Once it had happened, it seemed totally and entirely right . . . We felt as if our hands were being guided as we wrote his name on the paper."

After his election, and before he appeared before the world, the new pope was formally asked by what name he wished to be known. For the first time in history, a pope chose two names: John Paul, in honor of his two immediate predecessors, John XXIII, and Paul VI.

"I have neither Pope John's wisdom of heart nor the preparation and culture of Pope Paul," he said. "But I am in this place and so I must seek to serve the Church. I hope you will help me with your prayers."

For his papal motto he chose a single word, *Humilitas*, explaining that while he did not claim to excel in humility, he wished to commit himself to that virtue during his reign.

He proceeded at once to do away with some of the pomp that for centuries had surrounded the figure of the pope. At his coronation he refused to wear the Triple Crown, preferring instead a bishop's miter. He shortened the ceremony and opened it to many thousands by celebrating the Mass in Saint Peter's Square, rather than in the basilica. He also refused to be carried in the *sedia gestatoria* — the portable throne — but relented when he realized that on foot his short stature prevented many people from seeing him.

As Church leaders prepared for a new style of papal rule, the world's media set out to explore the life and background of the man who had so unexpectedly become the successor of Saint Peter.

Albino Luciani was born on October 17, 1912, in Canale d'Agordo, northeastern Italy, in a region lying between Venice and the Austrian border. A sickly infant, he was baptized immediately by the midwife, who feared that he might not survive. Throughout his childhood he suffered from bronchitis and pneumonia. "My mother took me from doctor to doctor," he remembered later.

His mother, Bortola, worked as a nurse's assistant; his father, Giovanni, was a bricklayer who spent much of each year away from the family, working in Germany. Later, he got a job in a local glassworks. The couple had two sons, Albino and Edoardo, and a daughter, Antonia. Another son, Federico, died during childhood. A widower when he married Bortola, Giovanni also had two daughters from his previous marriage, both mentally handicapped.

Though hardworking, the Lucianis were poor. "We went hungry at times," Albino recalled. In the summer months the children went to school barefoot; during the rest of the year they wore wooden clogs.

His mother was the stronger character in the marriage; the future pope described her as "sweet, but very severe." A devout Catholic, she had a profound influence on her children. Giovanni, on the other hand, was a socialist with an anticlerical streak.

A sermon by a Capuchin friar first turned young Albino's thoughts toward the priesthood. For a time he considered becoming a Capuchin himself. However, it was to the junior seminary of the Belluno diocese at Feltre that the eleven-year-old went in 1923. Giovanni, despite his coolness toward the Church, made no objection. "We must make this sacrifice," he said. Eventually his wife won him back to the faith.

At Belluno's major seminary, Albino's loveable personality and razor-sharp mind made a deep impression on professors and fellow students alike. "He was always amiable, quiet, serene, unless you stated something that was inaccurate — then he was like a spring," one student recalled. "I learned that in front of him you had to speak carefully. Any muddled thinking, and you were in trouble!"

Home on vacation, he helped on the family smallholding, just as he had done as a schoolboy, leading the cow to the pasture and cutting the hay.

Ordained on July 7, 1935, Albino spent two years in parish work and teaching before being appointed vice rector of the major seminary. When he was given the title of monsignor, a friend suggested that he wear the customary red-trimmed cassock. "Oh, come on," Albino grinned, "You know I have no time for that kind of nonsense!"

Unlike some of their neighbors, the Luciani family remained steadily aloof from Mussolini's ruling Fascist Party. When war came, and Mussolini allied himself with Hitler, Albino's brother Edoardo went underground to fight with the anti-Fascist partisans. His sister Antonia acted as a courier between the partisans and their supporters in Belluno — of whom Albino himself was the undoubted leader.

"He gave a lot of advice on how they were to move," she said later. "He was involved a great deal. In fact, he wove the threads of the Catholic resistance in our town."

Early one morning, Albino's mother heard someone knocking at her door. She opened it to find a woman on her knees — the wife of a schoolmaster who had taught Albino as a boy.

Though not a Fascist at heart, the man had involved himself with the movement in order to help his career. On the previous evening a group of Communist partisans had taken him from his home, plainly intending to shoot him.

"Make Albino come to the town," his wife begged, in tears. "Only he can save my husband."

Albino hurried to the home of one of his cousins, who was himself a Communist. At first the cousin denied any knowledge of the teacher's arrest.

"Look, I know you people have got him," Albino told him. "I'm not going back until you release him." The cousin promised to see what he could do, and Albino returned home.

The hours passed, and tension grew. In the evening Albino went back to see if there was any news. He was told that a courier had been to the hiding place where the teacher was held. The next morning he was freed and was soon safe at home with his wife.

Meanwhile, Albino's busy life at the seminary continued. Placed in charge of religious education in the diocese, he wrote a book, *Catechism in Breadcrumbs*, which was much used in schools. In 1950 the Gregorian University in Rome awarded him a doctorate in sacred theology for a thesis on the nineteenth-century theologian Antonio Rosmini.

Though his health remained delicate — he spent two spells in a tuberculosis sanitarium — in 1954 Albino became vicar general of the diocese, where he made his mark as a wise and humane administrator. When an overzealous pastor put a notice on his church door forbidding entry to women in short-sleeved dresses, and refusing Holy Communion to those wearing lipstick, Albino ordered him to remove it.

During a visit to Belluno, the patriarch of Venice, Cardinal Angelo Roncalli, quickly realized that here was a priest of outstanding gifts. When the neighboring diocese of Vittorio

Veneto fell vacant, the former Cardinal Roncalli, now Pope John XXIII, consecrated Albino its bishop at Saint Peter's on December 15, 1958.

Twice Albino declined the promotion, begging to be allowed to continue his work at Belluno. After the second refusal, Pope John summoned him to the Vatican, where Albino pleaded that his indifferent health — which at times involved difficulty in breathing — made him an unsuitable candidate. Beaming, the pope assured him that the mountain air of Vittorio Veneto would be good for him. And so it proved.

His smiling warmth and his total lack of pomp quickly won the hearts of priests and layfolk, just as, later on, it would win the hearts of people across the world. To everyone, he was simply "Don Albino." Visiting parishes, he dressed as a simple priest — a custom he continued later as patriarch of Venice. His brother Edoardo, a schoolteacher, commented: "As soon as he arrived anywhere, he struck up a friendship immediately."

During his earlier days as bishop, people often failed to recognize Albino. Mingling with a group in one parish, he asked whom they were waiting for. "For the bishop," they told him. "But it looks as though he's late."

"Oh, I don't think so," said Albino. "I believe I saw him arrive a little while ago."

Driving to say an early Mass one cold and rainy morning, he spotted a woman and her young son hurrying along the country road, heads bent against the wind. When he stopped to offer them a lift, they accepted gratefully. The woman agitatedly told him that she was to sing in the choir at the bishop's Mass, while her son was to carry the episcopal crosier.

"We're late; we should be there already," she said.

When the procession entered the church with Albino, vested, at the rear, he quickly spotted his lady passenger, who looked highly embarrassed.

"You see, we all got here on time," he smiled.

Young people he loved especially. "I am always happy with children," he said once. "Other people bring me problems, problems..."

He had his share of problems at Vittorio Veneto. In 1962 two priests got involved in a scam that cost numerous small investors their savings — two billion lire in total.

Bishop Albino called a meeting of his four hundred priests and announced that the diocese must repay every single lire. He also declared that the law must take its course — there would be no attempt to claim immunity. In the event, one priest served a year in jail; his companion was acquitted. Meanwhile Albino told the assembled clergy that he proposed to sell the diocesan treasure and also one of its buildings. He asked for their agreement and received it immediately.

"In this scandal there is a lesson for us all," he said. "We must be a poor Church."

Whenever he had to discipline a priest for any reason, he spent a sleepless night afterward. "I carry in my heart all the sorrow I have had to cause to the man I have disciplined," he told a friend.

Like many bishops, he more than once saw one of his priests leave the priesthood. Whenever this happened he took it badly, weeping and asking himself where he had gone wrong.

But it was not only the cares of his diocese that occupied his mind. Always a voracious reader — Mark Twain, Charles Dickens, and Walter Scott were among his favorite authors — Bishop Albino kept a file of newspaper and magazine cuttings on topics that interested him. "If I weren't a bishop, I should be a journalist," he would tell friends.

It was natural that he should be keenly aware of the Third World and its problems. In 1966 he traveled to Burundi, in East Africa, where he had "twinned" Vittorio Veneto with the

Karemba diocese, sending regular help. Driving along the rough African roads, his car swerved to avoid another vehicle and got stuck in mud at the roadside. The bishop got out and helped his companions to push it free.

On December 15, 1969, eleven years to the day after his ordination as bishop of Vittorio Veneto, Albino Luciani became patriarch of Venice. Once again he spurned the pomp that went with the office, including the traditional procession down the Grand Canal. On pastoral visits he traveled by *vaporetto*, the little waterbuses that carry ordinary citizens along the canals on their daily business.

Within days of his arrival, an army of poor folk descended on his residence seeking help — drunkards, beggars, and aged ex-prostitutes among them. He greeted each one individually and told them: "The patriarch's door is always open. Just ask Don Mario for anything you need."

Don Mario, his secretary, was horrified. "Your Excellency, I won't be able to look after them all," he whispered. "They'll ruin us."

The patriarch smiled. "Someone will help us," he said. Nobody was ever turned away: Many a newly released prisoner got a job and a new life thanks to the patriarch.

Visiting hospitals, he cheered patients with his smiles and jokes, but was disturbed by the honor guard of doctors, nurses, nuns, and officials who insisted on accompanying him around the wards. "Don't let me take up your precious time," he would beg, "I'll be fine on my own."

"But it's a privilege for us!" they protested. They failed to realize that he wanted his visits to be informal, and the patients to see him as what he was first and foremost — a priest. In time he learned to arrive on Sunday evenings, when there were fewer staff around, and he could tour without the usual procession trailing along behind.

In Venice, as in his previous diocese, he had to make some tough decisions. He dealt firmly with priests who became politically involved with left-wing parties, forbade "worker priests" to take jobs in factories, and disbanded the Catholic Student Federation because of its stance on the divorce issue.

When a tornado hit the Venetian lagoon, killing people sailing and camping along the shore, the patriarch hurried to the scene and spent the night consoling survivors and grieving relatives, and blessing bodies in the morgue.

On the next day he was due to visit a parish that had an annual procession in honor of Our Lady, to celebrate a local feast. Albino kept his promise to say Mass, but begged to be excused from the procession and other festivities. "I must go home to pray and to weep," he told the congregation.

One day a parish priest telephoned while he was eating lunch. The nun who answered asked him to call back later. When Albino heard about the call, he reproved the nun gently, telling her that in the future, she must always let him know that he was needed. "If a priest calls the patriarch at lunchtime, it must be urgent," he said.

Once, when he had sent the nuns who looked after him for a day out, they returned to find that the patriarch had cooked their evening meal.

"Each of us has a small talent for something," he said. "We ought to use it now and again."

Despite his prowess in the kitchen, the senior nun, Sister Vincenza, complained that the patriarch himself ate "like a canary," though he liked a glass of wine with his dinner. When she thought he looked tired, she would send him to bed. "It's Sister Vincenza who rules," he smiled.

Not everyone liked his simplicity. Venice's socialist mayor, Mario Rigo, confessed that he often found it disconcerting. One Catholic malcontent wrote to the Vatican to complain that he didn't visit parishes often enough, that he was over-familiar with people, and that he didn't know how to be a patriarch.

"I believe that I have visited the parishes regularly and have always returned gladly when invited," Albino replied. "I do have the habit of treating everyone as a brother. And thirdly, you are right — I don't know how to be a patriarch."

If Albino did not rate himself highly, one person in the Vatican had no doubt about his qualities. Visiting Venice in 1972, Pope Paul VI publicly placed his own red stole around the patriarch's shoulders, a gesture many interpreted as a sign that he wished Albino to succeed him. In the next year, the pope made him a cardinal.

Meanwhile, Albino was forming his own views on who should follow Pope Paul. He confided to an African cardinal that he thought the next pope should be a non-Italian. Visiting Brazil, he was deeply impressed by the Franciscan Cardinal Lorscheider, whom he saw as a likely candidate because of his spiritual and intellectual qualities, but most of all "because his mind and heart are with the poor."

At the 1971 Synod of Bishops, he proposed that dioceses in the affluent countries of the West should donate one percent of their income to those in the developing countries, a donation to be known as the "brothers' share." This, he added, "should not be given as charity, but as something owed, to compensate for the injustice being committed by the consumer world against the developing world." The synod did not accept his proposal.

In 1976 the patriarch sold a gold cross and chain that had been given to him by Pope John to raise money for spastic children, and he urged his priests to sell their church valuables and give the money to those who needed it. Few did.

Had Albino lived, justice toward the world's poor, and especially the redistribution of Church wealth, would undoubtedly have featured strongly in his pontificate.

Despite all the cares and pressures of his life as bishop and patriarch, Albino found time to write a number of books and pamphlets that demonstrate both simple faith and wide culture. In *My Rosary*, he deals frankly with the objections of sophisticated Catholics who find the Rosary boring, admitting that it can be unless undertaken in the right spirit.

"Personally, when I speak alone with God and Our Lady, rather than as a grownup I prefer to feel myself a child," he writes. "The miter, the skullcap, and the ring all disappear. I send the adult on vacation... And I abandon myself to the spontaneous tenderness that a child feels for his mom and dad."

His most famous work, *Illustrissimi*, consists of imaginary conversations with personalities from literature and history, ranging from Quintillian to Pinocchio. To Mark Twain he confides his own perception of his role:

"Just as there are different books, there are different bishops. Some are like eagles who glide at great heights with magnificent documents; others are like skylarks that sing the praises of the Lord in a marvelous way; finally, others are poor wrens that, on the lowest branch of the Church tree, only squeak, trying to express some thought on the broadest themes. I, Mark Twain, belong to the last category."

During a visit to Portugal in 1977, Albino went to see Sister Lucia, the survivor of the three Fatima visionaries, in the Carmelite convent at Coimbra. Afterward he would only say that he found her very talkative, but friends and relatives noticed that whenever the visit was mentioned, he grew quiet and appeared troubled. Both his brother and his sister believed afterward that Lucia may have prophesied that he would be the next pope.

The following year saw the death of Pope Paul, and the conclave to elect a successor. As it became clear that Albino was likely to emerge with the necessary two-thirds majority, Cardinal Sin of Manila told him: "You will be the new pope."

Later, when the Filipino cardinal knelt before him to pay homage, Albino told him: "You were a prophet, but my reign will be a short one."

It has been suggested that Sister Lucia may also have foretold his early death, but there could be a less dramatic explanation. Soon after Albino's election, his sister Antonia, a bricklayer's wife, warned the world in a media interview that his health was not good. Albino himself may have doubted whether it was strong enough to withstand the pressures of his new office.

Meanwhile, receiving Antonia for the first time as pope, he hugged her and chuckled: "Just think what Mom would say if she were here!"

As a seminarian, Albino had been raised in a conservative theological tradition that taught that "error has no rights." At the Second Vatican Council, which he attended as a bishop, he became firmly committed to its ideals, which he felt were not being realized as they should be. In his first address to the world as pope, he set out a six-point program:

1. to renew the Church through the norms of Vatican II,
2. to revise canon law,
3. to remind the Church of its foremost duty — to preach the Gospel,
4. to do everything possible to promote Church unity without watering down doctrine,
5. to promote dialog among all mankind, and
6. to promote and encourage all efforts for world peace and social justice.

Preparing to meet a group of American bishops, the new pope told his Irish secretary, Msgr. John Magee, that he would address them in Latin, because he did not feel that his English was equal to the occasion. Assured that it was quite good enough, the pope nevertheless rehearsed the short address four times and had Msgr. Magee celebrate Mass privately in English, with himself as altar server and reader, before facing his American audience.

Though such addresses were delivered in traditionally formal language, the pope's general audiences were much more relaxed, though spiced with quotes from authors ranging from Dante to Jules Verne. At his first audience, when he talked about the respect due to parents, he invited a young boy onto the platform to help him make his points.

Though the pope remained vigorous and cheerful, his staff noticed that his ankles were swollen. On the evening of September 29, he complained to Msgr. Magee that he was suffering from a severe headache, but said later that it had passed off.

Early the following morning, he was found dead in bed.

Within days, wild rumors about the cause of his death spread across the world. Several books appeared, purporting to show that the pope had been murdered by senior Church figures who feared that he was about to deal drastically with their real or alleged misdeeds. Differing public statements in the shocked aftermath of the death did nothing to stop the rumor mill: They conflicted on such detail as who first entered the pope's room, and what he had been reading when he died.

The conspiracy theories were powerfully refuted by the British writer John Cornwell, who was given access to those in the Vatican who were closest to the pope. In his book, *A Thief in the Night,* he showed conclusively that Pope John Paul I died from natural causes.

Soon after his death, the papal chamberlain, Cardinal Confalonieri, described John Paul I as a comet who flashed high across the sky, briefly lighting up the Church and the world.

Though the world's memory of the smiling pope has inevitably faded, many still pray to him and work to promote his cause.

12

"I CANNOT RISK
LOSING GOD"

Saint Josephine Bakhita

The girls were startled when the Arabs appeared suddenly from the barley field. Why were these men, both strangers, lurking there among the tall grain?

The older of the two smiled smoothly.

"Do not be afraid, little ones," he said. "We are only two poor travelers. We have come far across the Sudan — and we still have a great way to go."

So gracious was his manner that fear left them at once. The younger girl, a nine-year-old, obeyed readily when the Arab asked her, as a great favor, to fetch the parcel that he had left under a tree nearby.

"It will save our legs," he explained.

Her companion, who was fifteen, should have been suspicious when the two men told her to wait further along the path, until the younger girl returned. But she did not suspect anything. She did as she was told.

Meanwhile, the nine-year-old had reached the tree. There was no parcel. She turned, puzzled. Both Arabs were standing behind her, knives at the ready.

"Make a sound and you are dead!"

That they meant it, she had no doubt. Her screams would bring the men of the village running, and they would make short work of the Arabs — if they caught them. But by that time, she herself would be a corpse. Better to keep quiet.

As they hurried through the waving barley, a jumble of questions cascaded through her mind. How had the men managed to creep up on her so quietly, without the villagers seeing them? Why had they taken only her? What were they going to do with her?

With sickening clarity a memory came back to her, of a day half-forgotten when she had been little more than a baby. Her mother had gone to the fields, leaving herself and her twin sister in the care of an older sister who was married. Suddenly there had been a terrible commotion, with the men shouting and running everywhere, the women crying, and her mother screaming out her despair across the village.

When they were told what had happened, the two little girls did not really understand, but they cried anyway. Without anyone seeing them, Arabs like these had crept into the village and taken their married sister away. They never saw her again.

How would her mother stand this second terrible blow, the child wondered, as the men finally stopped and faced her?

"Tell us, my dear, what is your name?"

The elder man tried to smile reassuringly. He did not succeed. The little prisoner, half-paralyzed with fear, stared at her captor without replying.

"It doesn't matter," the man told her. "We'll give you a new name. From now on you will be called Bakhita. It's a nice name. It means the Lucky One."

But there's nothing lucky about me, thought Bakhita, as she lay in a locked hut with seven other captives. She knew now what her fate was to be. All of them were destined for the slave market.

In nineteenth-century Sudan, slavery was a thriving, highly organized industry. Its victims, generally black like Bakhita herself, would often pass through the hands of two or three middlemen before finding a permanent owner.

After spending a night in the bare, windowless hut, the victims were chained together and shepherded across the desert toward the rendezvous, where a dealer would be waiting to strike a bargain with their captors. Three of the prisoners were men and three women. The seventh was a girl of Bakhita's own age.

As the sun rose in the sky, Bakhita thought once more of the parents she had left behind and of the home she might never see again. She was unhappy and she was afraid, but her spirit was not broken. She resolved that if the chance came, she would escape.

Had her captors known what she was planning, they would have laughed. A mere child, and a negro child at that, run away into the unknown! No, Bakhita was born to be a slave — Allah had willed it — and a slave she would remain.

So they did not think they were taking any risk when, during a pause in the journey, they took the chains from the two young girls and left them to winnow some corn. In no time at all, the pair of them were off into the forest.

They wandered for several miles, not knowing where they were heading, hoping that somehow they would find the road home. What they found was a prowling lion.

Once again, there was no panic. From earliest childhood, they had been taught exactly what to do when faced with a danger like this. Scrambling swiftly up the nearest tree, the two stayed there until the lion grew tired of waiting and padded off to seek dinner elsewhere.

Their next encounter was with a prowling Arab — and this time, their luck was out. The girls readily accepted his offer of a meal, only to find themselves, just as before, locked in a hut. Their escape had been in vain; in the morning they were sold to the agent of another slave merchant. Soon they were once again part of a chain gang, plodding along to the slave market of El Obeid.

This time they were closely guarded; there was no chance to break for freedom. When they reached El Obeid, the merchant himself took a fancy to Bakhita and gave her to his daughter. So the little peasant became a lady's maid.

It was not a bad life, as slavery goes. With her gentle yet dignified manner and her sunny smile, Bakhita soon made herself popular. For a while, she was treated well.

Then, one day, Bakhita had the ill luck to break an ornamental vase belonging to the merchant's son, a spoiled, ill-tempered lout whose tantrums governed the household. Flying into a rage, he thrashed Bakhita soundly and demanded that his father get rid of her.

In her next home, she was miserable indeed. Her owner was a local Turkish officer, a henpecked man who might himself have been a slave for all the respect his womenfolk showed him. They seem to have been sadistically inclined, and Bakhita was completely at their mercy. They flogged her regularly and tattooed her simply to gratify a fashionable whim. Sometimes she suffered even at the officer's hands, for when his wife and daughters riled him, he took it out on the slaves.

Her luck changed again when her owner, traveling home to Turkey on leave, decided to sell off the slaves in Khartoum. Bakhita was bought by the Italian vice consul, Callisto Legnani, who treated her as a daughter while he tried to find out who her parents were so that he could send her back home. His efforts came to nothing — by this time Bakhita had forgotten her original name. So he took her back with him to Italy.

At the hotel in Genoa, Bakhita and her guardian became friendly with a rich lady named Signora Michieli. The signora's small daughter became so fond of the young Sudanese girl that the kindly vice consul agreed to give her into their care. So, at age fourteen, Bakhita found herself once more with a new owner.

The Michieli family owned a hotel at Suakim, on the Red Sea, and the plan was that Bakhita should eventually become a waitress there. She spent several months at the hotel with her mistress, but for the next six years she lived mainly at the family home near Venice, acting as companion to the little girl.

Just as she was about to move back to Suakim, the family steward stepped in with an unexpected request. Bakhita, nominally a Muslim, had received no instruction in the Christian faith. Should she not, he asked, remain in Italy long enough to learn something of it and then, if she wished, receive baptism?

Signor Michieli was a lapsed Catholic, and his wife Greek Orthodox. Nevertheless, they agreed that Bakhita's departure be delayed. As Signora Michieli prepared to travel without her, the young daughter, Mimmina, announced that she could not bear to be parted from her beloved companion even for a few months. So she, too, stayed behind, and it was arranged that both girls should board at the Venice convent of the Daughters of Charity of Canossa.

Centuries before Bakhita's time, before Islam swept through the Middle East, much of the Sudan had been Christian; early travelers spoke wonderingly of its churches and monasteries. Bakhita's people, the Daju, ruled over a stretch of territory in Darfur, where black Africa meets the Arab world. Her ancestors may, therefore, have been Christian — but Bakhita knew nothing of that. She only knew, when she entered the convent, that at last she had come home.

When Signora Michieli returned ten months later to reclaim the girl, whom she still regarded as her property, an unpleasant surprise awaited her. Nothing short of physical force, Bakhita declared, would ever make her leave the Canossian sisters.

The illiterate slave girl, pushed around all her life, now showed a dignity and strength of purpose that amazed everyone around her. All the pride and breeding of her ancient race asserted itself — but there was more to her newfound determination than that. At the convent, Bakhita had learned well. If Christ's teaching were true, she demanded, how could anyone claim to own her body and soul?

The mother superior, who at first had sided with Signora Michieli, began to have serious misgivings. Might not Bakhita, after all, be right? Signora Michieli was a good woman, certainly; but could she really lay claim to Bakhita as her slave?

Clearly this was a case for higher authority, for the cardinal patriarch himself. Because civil law also was involved, the patriarch called in the king's procurator. Two days later, these high representatives of Church and State held court in the convent parlor to decide Bakhita's fate.

The hearing was heated, with Signora Michieli and her friends loudly demanding that the wayward slave girl return with them to Suakim.

When Bakhita was invited to speak, she was brief — yet no lawyer could have bettered her argument.

"I love the signora dearly," she said, "and to part from Mimmina cuts me to the heart. But I shall not leave this place because I cannot risk losing God."

Cardinal Agostini had no doubts about Bakhita's case, but the final verdict rested with the procurator. He did not have any doubts either. Because slavery was illegal under Italian law, he declared, any slave was emancipated immediately when he or she touched Italian soil. Bakhita was a free woman, and nobody would be allowed to interfere with her rights.

Mimmina was heartbroken, her mother furious. "Give that ungrateful girl a kiss, then forget her," she commanded. "You will never see her again."

On January 9, 1890, the former slave girl was baptized by the cardinal patriarch, with a countess for her godmother and a great crowd of well-wishers all eager to welcome her into the Church. They gasped when she appeared, radiant in her purple dress and black veil — the veil being exchanged for a white one as soon as the water had been poured on her forehead.

It was not the affection of these people, or of the nuns who looked after her, that Bakhita found most wonderful. Could it really be true, she asked again and again, that in God's eyes she was someone who mattered, someone He cared for at every moment of her life? Sometimes she would hurry to the nearest available sister just to be reassured once more.

In the end, she was convinced. She, Bakhita, was someone important; as important as Signora Michieli, as important as the cardinal patriarch — even as important as the mother superior. And so she became a Christian, with three new names: Josephine, Margaret Fortunata. The last one was not, of course, really new. It was simply the Italian version of the name her Arab captors had given her, so long ago it seemed now: Fortunata — the lucky one.

From the beginning she wanted to become a Canossian sister, but it was some time before she plucked up the courage to ask to be accepted as a postulant. A black Christian might be all very fine, but who ever heard of a black nun?

This was a reasonable question: In the Europe of those days, black religious were few indeed. When she did eventually confide her wish, she was assured that black nuns were just as acceptable as white ones. The mother superior, though delighted by her request, was not surprised. She knew from the beginning that Bakhita had a vocation, but refrained from approaching her because she did not wish to influence her in any way. The decision to enter had to be entirely her own.

So Bakhita became a Canossian sister and remained one for more than fifty years, cheerfully performing any task she was given, with a kind word and a big smile for everyone.

"Don't you have any passions like the rest of us?" asked one sister, amazed at her constant equanimity.

"Of course I have," replied Bakhita, with that familiar grin. "But when they trouble me I just say, 'Go away now and I'll attend to you later.'"

The terrible traumas of her childhood left no mark on her personality, a fact that might well surprise a psychiatrist. Her secret was, undoubtedly, that ever-present sense of God's love.

"If I had known it when I was a slave," she said, "I would never have suffered so much."

She bore not the slightest resentment toward those who had caused her to suffer: quite the reverse.

"If I were to meet the slave traders who kidnapped me and even those who tortured me, I would kneel and kiss their hands," she declared. "For if that had not happened, I would not be a Christian and a religious today."

She wanted very much to return to the Sudan, to find her family, and if possible, to help in the conversion of her compatriots.

"They are really good out there," she would say often. "They would make such fervent Christians." And she prayed: "O Lord, if I could fly to my people and tell them of your goodness at the top of my voice, oh, how many souls would be saved."

Her wish was never granted. Instead her superiors had her travel the length and breadth of Italy, rallying support for the missions at meetings often attended by bishops and other dignitaries.

"Be good! Love God! Pray for the pagans!" She always ended her talks with these words, and they must have struck home to many.

In some towns there were traffic jams because of the crowds who turned out to hear her. They would have been surprised, looking at her always-smiling face, to know how the famous Mother Josephine really felt about her lecture tours.

"No doubt everyone thought I was enjoying myself," she confided years later, "but for me, they were a slow martyrdom."

Yet she went on giving of her best, because that was what obedience demanded, and because she knew that she was helping the people of Africa who were so close to her heart.

For most of her long life, Bakhita enjoyed excellent health, but in the last four years she suffered a barrage of ailments that slowly reduced her to absolute helplessness and cruelly disfigured her once-attractive face. Her mind, however, remained unimpaired and so did her radiant personality.

Her greatest suffering was the trouble she caused to others, though none of the sisters begrudged the care they gave her. When they scolded her for not calling when she needed help, she replied with a smile: "Since I can no longer keep the Rule myself, the least I can do is let the rest of you keep it."

Sisters who came to her room to comfort "poor" Mother Josephine soon found their own spirits being lifted by the ever-cheerful patient. Brushing aside all talk of her own ailments, she demanded news of everything and everyone. When she did mention her illness, it was usually to joke about it.

"I'm all skin and bone — there'll be nothing left for the worms," she said, as disease wasted her away. She died on February 8, 1947, at Schio, close to the Italian Alps. As she uttered her last words, "Our Lady! Our Lady!" a wonderful smile lit up her face.

She had lived at the convent there for many years, and the townsfolk regarded her as their own. They still call her "our black Mother." Her funeral was more a triumphal procession than a solemn farewell, and the splendid marble monument later erected over her grave, with its florid recital of her virtues, would certainly have made her chuckle.

Bakhita was beatified by Pope John Paul II on May 17, 1992, and canonized on October 1, 2000. No more colorful story appears in these pages than hers, and yet we should not let that blind us to her true importance. She is a saint not because her early life was dramatic, but rather because of the holiness she gained during the long, undramatic years that followed.

13

"WE ARE PROPHETS
OF A FUTURE NOT OUR OWN"

Archbishop Oscar Romero

At 6:25 on the evening of March 24, 1980, Archbishop Oscar Romero of San Salvador was saying a memorial Mass at the city's Hospital of Divine Providence for a journalist friend's mother who had recently died.

He read to the congregation from Saint John's gospel: "The hour has come for the Son of Man to be glorified . . . Unless the grain of wheat falls to the earth and dies, it remains only a grain. But if it dies, it bears much fruit."

The archbishop took up the theme in his homily, applying it to the misery being inflicted on his country, El Salvador, by its murderous rulers.

"It's important not to love ourselves so much that we are not willing to take the risks that history demands of us," he told the little congregation. "Those who try to fend off the danger will lose their lives. But whoever out of love for Christ gives himself to the service of others will live, like the grain of wheat that dies, but only apparently dies."

The ten-minute homily drew to a close. From the nearby kitchen came the muffled sound of pots and pans as nuns prepared the evening meal for the patients. In a moment the archbishop would move to the center of the altar to offer the bread and wine for Christ's sacrifice.

Suddenly, a shot rang out from the rear of the chapel. Archbishop Romero slumped to the floor behind the altar, at the foot of the large crucifix. As some of the congregation crouched in fear, others ran forward to his aid, nuns among them. Of the gunman there was no sign.

They turned the wounded man onto his back. Blood poured from his mouth and nose, staining his violet chasuble and white alb. The bullet, piercing his left breast, had lodged in one of his right ribs. It had fragmented, causing heavy internal bleeding. He was deeply unconscious.

The little cancer hospital had no emergency room, so they drove him to the Policlinica Hospital — a five-minute journey in the speeding ambulance. As staff struggled to begin a blood transfusion, Archbishop Romero gave a final gasp and died.

Though his life had been threatened many times, the murder sent shock waves through El Salvador and around the world. Since he became archbishop three years before, Oscar Romero had spoken out fearlessly against a social system that kept millions in grinding poverty while a privileged few controlled the country's wealth. Each Sunday morning the entire nation listened to his broadcast sermons denouncing the death squads who daily left tortured, bullet-ridden bodies at roadsides, on garbage dumps, and in ditches.

For nearly one hundred years, the tiny Central American republic had been ruled by the military, backed by an oligarchy of wealthy families who owned most of the land and ran the country's industries. The poorest in El Salvador were the *campesinos*, the rural peasants who worked mainly in the coffee and sugar plantations.

In the first left-wing uprising, in 1932, the army slaughtered thirty thousand people. By the mid-1970s political murder was rife across the nation. The death squads picked off anyone whose views seemed to threaten the established order. Some were snatched from their homes, or from the streets, and were found dead later. Others simply disappeared, never to be seen again.

For centuries the Church in El Salvador, as elsewhere, regarded social inequalities as the will of God, and exhorted the poor to accept their lot patiently. Any attempt at political activity was discouraged or condemned outright. Oscar Romero was trained in this tradition, and in his early years he upheld it.

"He was a friend of the poor and a friend of the rich," one of his parishioners remembered.

"To the rich he would say, 'Love the poor,' and he would tell us poor to love God, and that God knew what he was doing by putting us last in line, and that afterward we would be assured a place in heaven. He would preach to us about the heaven where rich people who gave alms would go, and where poor people who didn't cause too much trouble would go."

Young Father Romero's rise in the Church was assured. Hardworking, intellectually gifted, a devoted pastor, and a man of prayer, he was clearly headed for a bishop's miter in a country that produced few native-born priests. What none could have foreseen, in those early days, was the radical change in his vision of the Gospel, and the way in which he would live and, in the end, die for it.

Oscar Arnulfo Romero y Galdámez was born on August 15, 1917, at Ciudad Barrios in the department of San Miguel, a remote region of El Salvador close to the border with Honduras. His father, Santos, was the town's telegrapher and postmaster. His mother, Guadalupe de Jesús, bore Santos eight children, of whom one, a girl, died as a baby. Oscar was the second in the family. Santos, afterward described as "not pious," also fathered several illegitimate children around the town.

Like their neighbors, the Romeros were poor. There was no electricity, and beds were shared. Along with his brothers and his surviving sister, Oscar delivered letters and telegrams and learned to send telegraph messages. At twelve or thirteen he was apprenticed to a local carpenter, who remembered him as a serious boy, the best of his apprentices, who often stopped after work to pray at one of the town's two churches.

At fourteen Oscar entered the minor seminary at San Miguel, and in 1937 he went on to the national seminary in San Salvador, where he stayed for only seven months before being sent to Rome to complete his studies. He was ordained there on April 4, 1942.

A strong swimmer from his earliest years, he taught a number of his fellow students to swim during summer breaks.

After ordination he began work on a doctorate in ascetical theology, but returned to El Salvador before he could complete it. There are varying explanations of this. One is that war conditions made it impossible to continue; another, that he was recalled because the country was short of priests. On the voyage home the ship stopped at Cuba, where he and a fellow priest were arrested and held in an internment camp for three months, until the Cuban authorities decided that they were not enemy aliens.

After a brief period as a village pastor, he was appointed secretary to the bishop of San Miguel and given charge of a city parish, San Francisco. Later he became pastor of the cathedral parish. His appetite for work awed friends and colleagues. He visited schools and jails, organized catechism classes, and oversaw several lay associations. His memory was phenomenal: One friend described him as "a walking library."

When he did relax, he watched films. On his jail visits he generally took a film with him to brighten the prisoners' lives. He also loved the circus, and was always in the audience whenever one came to town.

During these years he lived at the minor seminary with Father Rafael Valladares, the friend with whom he had studied in Rome and been detained in Cuba. Rafael edited the diocesan newspaper, a job Oscar later took over. While Rafael was cheerful and outgoing, Oscar was shy and retiring, though he was much more relaxed in the company of the young seminarians.

He also liked to joke with the city's shoeshine boys, whom he allowed to sleep in the cathedral if they had nowhere else to go. "See if you can make them squeak!" he would say, as they went to work on his shoes.

Oscar was a soft touch for anyone down on his luck. Each day he would meet with a lineup of drunks, prostitutes, and panhandlers, handing a coin to each one. "Be good!" he would tell them, probably without much hope.

Priests who were lax got the rough side of his tongue, which did not make him popular. He also made enemies among Protestants, whom he criticized in broadcast sermons. By refusing Christian burial to Freemasons, he antagonized some of the rich and influential families in the city.

Although he absorbed and publicly upheld the teachings of the Second Vatican Council, he was unhappy with some of the trends that followed it. He disapproved especially of "sloppy priests" who went around without their cassocks.

As liberation theology spread through Latin America, inspiring priests and peasants to fight against social injustice, he worried about what he saw as the increasing politicization of the Church. Like others, he feared that Christ was being turned into a left-wing revolutionary leader. He was naturally suspicious of the new base communities: Bible study groups that applied the Gospel to the social situation and gave to lay people leadership roles that were previously exercised only by priests.

In 1967 he was appointed secretary of the national bishops' conference, which meant a move to the capital, San Salvador, where he went to live in the national seminary. Later he took on additional responsibilities as executive secretary of the Episcopal Council for Central America and Panama. Soon after celebrating his priestly silver jubilee, he was given the title of monsignor.

The seminary, his new home, was staffed by Jesuits. Romero did not like the way they ran the place. He was disturbed by the freedom given to the students and by the emphasis on liberation theology.

In his new role, Msgr. Romero was closely involved in preparations for the historic conference of the Latin American bishops at Medellin, Colombia, in 1968. Here the bishops decided to cut their links with powerful ruling groups in favor of a "preferential option for the poor." Afterward some noticed that Romero was visibly uncomfortable whenever Medellin was mentioned. Apparently he thought it was a further move in the Marxist direction.

In 1970 Oscar Romero was ordained as auxiliary bishop to Archbishop Chavez of San Salvador. Among the attending dignitaries was the president of El Salvador, Fidel Sanchez Hernandez.

Not everyone was happy at his promotion. A group of progressive priests, based at the National University, wrote a public letter denouncing him as a conservative who was trying to block the Church's movement toward renewal. Unfazed, Bishop Romero used the archdiocesan newspaper to attack two Jesuits who were giving spiritual exercises to diocesan clergy. He alleged that the exercises were in fact classes in Marxist sociology.

In 1972 the people of El Salvador voted massively for a coalition of center and left-wing parties and against the ruling PCN (*Partido de Conciliacíon Nacional*), the party of the military. It made no difference to anything. The army, as always, had the last word, and Colonel Arturo Armando Molina was installed as the new president.

Widespread protests followed. At El Carmen, in Romero's home province of San Miguel, soldiers snatched twelve *campesinos* from their homes. The following day, Good Friday, their bodies were found dumped at the entrance to the village.

In the capital itself Molina ordered troops into the National University, where they badly beat protesters and arrested eight hundred of them. Romero, on behalf of the bishops' conference, publicly backed the invasion on the ground that the university was a hotbed of subversion.

Archbishop Chavez, a man of Medellin, became increasingly unhappy at his auxiliary's reactionary stance and resolved to try to broaden his outlook. Two priests who worked in the countryside with the *campesinos* had been accused by local landowners of plotting an uprising. Forced to lie low for a time, they decided that the trouble had died down and that it was time to return to their base in a village outside the city. The archbishop asked Romero to make the journey with one of the priests, Inocencio Alas.

At a checkpoint they were stopped by police, who demanded to see their papers and insisted on searching the car. Forced to drive with the officers to the local police headquarters, they were accused of being Communists and threatened with arrest. They were released only after Romero demanded to phone President Molina and showed the police chief his pocketbook containing the direct-line number to the presidential desk.

It was the auxiliary bishop's first taste of the oppression suffered by so many of his fellow countrymen.

In November 1974 there was another massacre, this time at La Cayetana in the San Vicente diocese, when soldiers and police killed six *campesinos*, beat two of their widows, and robbed a number of homes. Thirteen other men disappeared. All the dead men were catechists trained in leadership courses run by the Passionists at Los Naranjos. The bishops' conference denounced the outrage.

The protest had no effect. Seven months later six more *campesinos*, all from one family, were shot and hacked to death at Tres Calles, in the diocese of Santiago de Maria, by soldiers who claimed that they were searching for weapons and had been fired upon. Again, the murdered men were catechists trained at Los Naranjos.

The next day, the bishop of the diocese went to the village to console their families. The bishop was Oscar Romero, who had been installed a fortnight after the massacre at El Carmen.

He protested to the local army commander and to President Molina, believing that it was best to proceed through official channels. No matter who the victims were or what they had done, he said, they were still entitled to justice and should not have been summarily executed.

Yet he was still troubled by progressive trends in the Church, and especially suspicious of the Passionists and the courses they taught. His eyes were soon to be opened.

Each year an army of *campesinos* flooded into the area to gather the coffee harvest. Realizing that they were sleeping in the open during the cold nights, he opened an old school building as a shelter and ordered that they be served hot drinks. Talking with them, he was shocked to find that many were paid a wage below the official minimum.

A Passionist priest explained that by registering some of the workers as "helpers," the foremen were able to pay them less. This was illegal, but government inspectors were bribed to ignore it. Romero went to a plantation and checked for himself. What the priest had told him was true. Now he was deeply shaken; among his friends were a number of rich coffee growers. Was this really how they got rich? And if the Passionists were training the *campesinos* to fight for a just wage, how could that be wrong?

When Oscar Romero was named archbishop of San Salvador in February 1977, there was widespread gloom among the base communities and the priests working with them, and among other progressive-minded Catholics. Some refused to attend his installation. There were letters of protest. One community wrote to the archbishop elect: "What is your message, *Monseñor*? We would like to know if you are going to stand with the rich, or with us, the poor?"

The retiring Archbishop Chavez was deeply disappointed. He had recommended that his auxiliary, Arturo Rivera, be appointed to succeed him. But Rome well knew that Rivera was regarded by the right wing and the military as a Marxist in a miter. Romero, on the other hand, was a man who wouldn't make waves.

As he prepared to take possession of the archdiocese, the government deported a number of the foreign priests working in El Salvador, including two from the United States. Some were tortured before being forced to cross the border into Guatemala, where they were thrown into jail.

A fortnight after Oscar Romero's appointment, the country got a new military ruler. General Carlos Humberto Romero (no relation) was named president after another fraudulent election. During the protests that followed, the army opened fire on a huge crowd demonstrating in San Salvador's Plaza Libertad. More than one hundred demonstrators were killed, and many more wounded. Others took refuge in El Rosario Church, on the plaza.

When the massacre occurred the new archbishop was out of town, winding up affairs in his former diocese. He returned immediately, and appeared bewildered by what had happened. Meanwhile, articles in government-sponsored newspapers angrily denounced the role of "Communist" clergy in stirring up trouble.

On March 12, Rutilio Grande, a dynamic Jesuit priest, was ambushed and killed by a death squad as he traveled from his home parish at Aguilares to say an evening Mass at El Paisnal, a few miles away. His two companions, an old man and a fifteen-year-old boy, died with him.

Archbishop Romero received the news in a phone call from Colonel Molina, the outgoing president, who rang to offer his condolences and to assure him that the government was not involved in the killing.

Romero was badly shaken. Despite his mistrust of the Jesuits, he and Rutilio had become friends in the days when he lived at the seminary and Rutilio belonged to its Jesuit community. The murdered priest had been master of ceremonies at his episcopal ordination in 1970.

Since 1972 Rutilio had headed a team of younger Jesuits working among the thirty thousand *campesinos* in the Aguilares district. The Jesuits trained many of them as lay leaders, and taught them to apply the lessons of the Bible to their own lives. In his sermons, Rutilio constantly decried a system that enabled rich landowners to exploit the poor and landless.

It was Rutilio's murder, more than any other single event, that changed Oscar Romero. After viewing the bodies, he wrote to the president to say that he would not attend any state function until the crime had been fully investigated. He also ordered that on Sunday, March 20, there would be only one Mass in the archdiocese, which he would concelebrate with all the clergy. In this way, Christians would show that they were united in their protest against government oppression.

On that Sunday morning, the cathedral was packed and more than one hundred thousand people crowded into the plaza outside. Before Mass began, priests came outside to hear confessions, and many lapsed Catholics returned to the faith that day. Those outside listened to the Mass on their radios.

In his sermon Archbishop Romero thanked them for their support, and for the support they gave to priests who, like Father Grande, risked the ultimate sacrifice. On hearing the murdered priest's name, the crowd exploded into applause.

"Who touches one of my priests touches me," declared the archbishop. "And they will have to deal with me."

A priest who was present said later: "I felt the Holy Spirit descend upon him."

Romero decided to go quickly to Rome to explain to the pope what was happening in El Salvador. This was especially urgent as he knew that the papal nuncio, Archbishop Gerada, was sending negative reports to the Vatican. Gerada was anxious to stay on the right side of the government.

Paul VI listened carefully, then took both Romero's hands. "*Coraggio!*" he said. "Take heart!"

Some of San Salvador's wealthy citizens offered him a big house and an expensive car. He declined both, and went to live in a tiny bungalow on the grounds of the hospital where he would later meet his death.

In the years that followed there was more bloodshed: Both priests and *campesinos* fell victim to the death squads. A slogan appeared on the streets: "Be a patriot — kill a priest." Among those who died was Octavio Ortiz, the first priest whom Romero had ordained after becoming a bishop, murdered while giving a retreat to a group of young men in the village of El Despertar. Four retreatants died with him, two of them only fifteen years old.

Despite the murders, and the threats to his own life, Romero continued to speak out on YSAX, the radio station operated by the archdiocese. Persecution, he told listeners, must be expected, even welcomed: "A Church that suffers no persecution, but enjoys the privileges and support of the things of the earth — beware! — is not the true Church of Jesus Christ."

Whatever happened, he assured them, the Church would endure: "If someday they take away the radio station from us . . . if they don't let us speak, if they kill all the priests and the bishop, too, and you are left a people without priests, each one of you must become God's microphone, each one of you must become a prophet."

To those who charged him with preaching a political gospel, he replied: "The Church is pointing out sin, and society must listen to that accusation and be converted and so become what God wants."

Despite this, four of his fellow bishops wrote to the Vatican with a string of accusations against him. These included fomenting class war, presenting Jesus Christ as a revolutionary leader, encouraging lay Catholics to oppose their bishops, and blessing terrorism.

The latter charge was particularly cruel and totally without foundation. Never at any time did Romero preach armed resistance. When guerillas from the Popular Liberation Forces (FPL) kidnapped El Salvador's foreign minister, Mauricio Borgonovo, Romero pleaded for his release. All appeals for mercy were in vain: Borgonovo was murdered. At his funeral Mass, the archbishop reiterated the Church's opposition to violence.

Though hurt by the accusations of his brother bishops, Romero continued to preach his message with as much vigor as ever: "This is the mission entrusted to the Church, a hard mission: to uproot sins from history; to uproot sins from the political order; to uproot sins from the economy; to uproot sins wherever they are."

Again and again he insisted on the Church's duty to demand changes in society. Unjust social structures, he declared, were at the root of all public violence and unrest.

"Many would like a preaching so spiritualistic that it leaves sinners unbothered and does not call idolaters those who kneel before money and power," he said. "A preaching that says nothing of the sinful environment . . . is not the Gospel."

When the United States government sent the ruling junta in El Salvador military equipment and experts and promised more, Romero appealed to President Carter to withdraw the aid, which would only lead to more injustice and repression. He got a conciliatory reply from Secretary of State Cyrus Vance, who assured him Washington was concerned that American aid not be used in a repressive manner.

Like another murdered archbishop, England's Thomas à Becket, Oscar Romero knew that he would face martyrdom. A fortnight before his death, he wrote: "I am bound as a pastor, by divine command, to give my life for those whom I love, and that is all Salvadorans, even those who are going to kill me."

On March 23, 1980, he made a direct appeal to the men of the armed forces:

"Brothers, you come from our own people. You are killing your own brothers. Any human order to kill must be subordinate to the law of God, which says, 'Thou shalt not kill.' No soldier is obliged to obey an order contrary to the law of God. No one has to obey an immoral law. It is high time you obeyed your consciences rather than orders. The Church cannot remain silent before such an abomination. ... In the name of God, in the name of this suffering people, whose cries rise to heaven more loudly each day, I implore you, I beg you, I command you: Stop the repression."

The appeal was his death warrant. The next morning, government-backed newspapers announced pointedly that he would say Mass that evening in the Hospital of Divine Providence. Friends begged him not to go, but he would not hear of it. He had promised. The Mass, which he was never to complete, was his last.

Despite the shock and anger that greeted his death worldwide, Archbishop Romero was not to be El Salvador's last martyr.

Less than nine months later, on December 2, 1980, four American missionaries, Maryknoll Sisters Ita Ford and Maura Clarke, Ursuline Sister Dorothy Kazel, and lay missionary Jean

Donovan, were stopped at an army checkpoint as they drove from San Salvador airport. Taken to a hidden spot nearby, they were abused and shot.

On November 16, 1989, six Jesuit priests, Ignacio Ellacuria, Segundo Montes, Ignacio Martin-Baro, Joaquin Lopez y Lopez, Juan Ramon Moreno, and Amado Lopez, were murdered by the military on the campus of the University of Central America in San Salvador. Their housekeeper, Elba Ramos, and her daughter, Celia Marisela Ramos, also were killed.

The international outrage that followed forced El Salvador's government to negotiate an end to the civil war that claimed more than seventy thousand victims in the 1980s and early 1990s. Oscar Romero, who never doubted that one day peace and justice would come to his country, left us this meditation:

> *It helps, now and then, to step back and take the long view.*
> *The kingdom is not only beyond our efforts, it is beyond our*
> *   vision.*
> *We accomplish in our lifetime only a tiny fraction*
> *of the magnificent enterprise that is God's work.*
> *Nothing we do is complete, which is another way of saying*
> *that the kingdom of God always lies beyond us.*
>
> *No statement says all that could be said.*
> *No prayer fully expresses our faith.*
> *No confession brings perfection.*
> *No pastoral visit brings wholeness.*
> *No program accomplishes the Church's mission.*
> *No set of goals and objectives includes everything.*
>
> *This is what we are about:*
> *We plant seeds that one day will grow.*

We water seeds already planted,
knowing that they hold future promise.
We lay foundations that will need further development.
We provide yeast that produces effects beyond our abilities

We cannot do everything,
and realizing that gives us a sense of liberation.
This enables us to do something and to do it very well.
It may be incomplete but it is a beginning, a step along
*   the way,*
an opportunity for God's grace to enter and do the rest.
We may never see the end results,
but that is the difference between the master builder and
*   the worker.*
We are workers, not master builders,
ministers, not messiahs.
We are prophets of a future not our own.
Amen.

14

"WE DO VERY LITTLE GOOD WHEN WE EMBARK ON OUR OWN"

Blessed Cyprian Tansi

It was a happy day in Nigeria — probably the happiest in the nation's history. More than half a million people gathered on the airfield at Oba, in the east of the country, to see Pope John Paul II beatify the first Nigerian ever to be so honored by the Church. Along the dusty roads they came by the thousands, many carrying children, chairs, or bundles of food and water on their heads; some walking all night. As dancers brandishing elephant tusks gyrated to the sound of drums, the pope declared that Cyprian Michael Iwene Tansi "shall hereafter be invoked as Blessed." The date: March 22, 1998.

Blessed Cyprian had died only thirty-four years before. Among those at the ceremony was his eighty-nine-year-old brother, Godwin. Many others present had known him; some of the bishops and priests taking part had discovered their vocations under his influence. Yet his death had not taken place here, in his homeland, but far away in England, where he spent the last fourteen years of his life behind monastery walls.

Born in the nearby village of Igboezunu in September 1903, Blessed Cyprian was named Iwene by his pagan parents, Tabansi and Ejikwevi. Like his three brothers and his sister, he was brought up to believe in voodoo.

Some time before Iwene's birth, Tabansi had been jailed by the ruling British authorities. We do not know the reason for this; possibly it involved some conflict between tribal custom and colonial law. Whatever the reason, Tabansi decided that his son should receive an education that would enable him to deal with the British on their own terms.

So at age six, Iwene was sent to live with a Christian aunt and uncle at Aguleri. His uncle was a teacher; Iwene was the only member of his family to go to school and to learn English. He soon showed himself to be an able and hardworking student, despite losing the sight in his left eye when another boy threw a lump of clay at him as a group of them were horsing around.

On January 7, 1912, he was baptized and took the name Michael. The eight-year-old went home and broke up his juju, the wooden fetish given to him at birth to ward off evil spirits.

From the time of his baptism, he showed remarkable piety. Friends wanting him to play with them outdoors would find him in the church, sometimes with tears running down his cheeks. Some of the boys made fun of him, others beat him up, while a third group tried to imitate him. Whatever they did, Michael prayed as fervently as ever, attending Mass each morning before school.

His simple and polite manners pleased his teachers. When one of them gave him a discarded raffia bag for his books, Michael was delighted. "For him it was an unforgettable present for which he never ceased thanking me," the teacher recalled.

At sixteen Michael graduated from high school, which made him eligible to teach. The following year he joined the staff of Holy Trinity School, Onitsha.

His students remembered him as kind but strict, caning those who misbehaved or were lazy. Lessons were mostly in Ibo, the tribal language of the area. A student who later became a bishop recalled that one day, when Michael spoke English to the class and they answered well, he was so pleased that he gave them three pence to spend on candy — a small sum, but a fortune to kids in a poor African village.

At nineteen, Michael was hit by a tragedy that influenced his life profoundly. After several children in his home village died, the local witch doctor decided that Michael's elderly mother, Ejikwevi, was sucking away their lives so that she could live. She was forced to drink a herbal poison, which killed her. Overcome by the barbarity of her death, the grief-stricken teenager resolved to do all in his power to win his fellow countrymen away from their pagan beliefs.

Meanwhile he continued to spend long hours in prayer, and he studied hard to improve his qualifications. In 1924, at age twenty-one, he was appointed principal of Saint Joseph's School, Aguleri, where he had graduated only five years before.

Though highly respected, the young principal was not popular with his colleagues. The teachers lived together, and Michael treated them almost as strictly as he did the pupils — so much so, that many were unwilling to work under him. Those who did complained that he expected them to live like hermits.

There was a cast-iron rule that no woman might enter a teacher's quarters — not even his mother. When one told him that this was going too far, he chuckled. "Your mother has no badge on her face to show that she is your mother," he said.

Ascetic in his own habits, he kept beer in the house for his guests but drank only water himself. Yet he was a cheerful and generous host, who laughed uproariously as he swapped jokes.

Two years after Michael's appointment as principal, a seminary for the Onitsha diocese opened at Igbariam, on the banks of the Niger River. Michael applied to enter, but had to wait for another two years until a new principal could be found for the school.

Life in the seminary was hard for everyone. There was only one professor instead of the five required by canon law, so studies were difficult and protracted. In addition to their studies, the seminarians worked in the fields and kept the building clean.

After several years as a student, Michael was appointed procurator, responsible for food and other needs. He would not tolerate any kind of waste: A new pencil was provided only after the user had presented the worn-down stub of the previous one. Although some students found this regime trying, most appreciated his obvious goodness. "This goodness was infectious, and so was his charity," wrote another future bishop.

His prowess on the soccer field also won admirers: Fast on his feet, he was a prolific goal-scorer. As in everything else, he threw himself wholeheartedly into the game, playing hard until the final whistle.

"He always undervalued himself, which, I think, is not a very common characteristic among his people," recalled the seminary rector, Spiritan Father Denis Kennedy. Shortly before he was to be ordained sub-deacon, Michael told Father Kennedy that he felt unworthy to go on to the priesthood, in particular, because he lacked the necessary knowledge.

Father Kennedy assured him that although he was not a great theologian, he knew enough Christianity to preach it to his people. Furthermore, he had the valuable advantage that he was an Ibo speaker. Emphasizing that the choice must be entirely his own, Father Kennedy assured Michael that if he decided to stay, he would certainly be ordained. Michael went away delighted.

On December 19, 1937, Michael Iwene Tansi was ordained a priest, along with two fellow students. His first appointment was as curate at Nnewi, where he spent the next two years.

"Father Michael was the most hardworking of all the priests who ever lived at Nnewi, and he hardly ate because time spent at table could be utilized doing some work," a parishioner remembered. "He was regarded as a living saint."

He repaired thatched churches with the men and scrubbed floors with the women. He gave money to the destitute from his own meager income and took particular care of the lepers, who were shunned by most of the population.

In 1939 he was appointed pastor of a new parish based at Dunukofia, a village with a few dilapidated houses. A teacher, also newly appointed, was shocked when he saw Michael's quarters. "He was living in a wretched hut — it would not be good enough for my chickens today," he said.

With his usual energy, Michael set about transforming Dunukofia and the neighboring villages included in the parish. Soon there was a new church. "He got each village at work on a building. Even pagans and elders came along," recalled yet another future bishop.

Michael himself planned and built houses and schools, painted walls, and polished furniture, teaching those who helped him how to do the job well. He gathered the orphans, fed them, and sent them to school. Some of them went on to become teachers.

Training young people for marriage was a major concern. He thought it important that the future mothers of Christian families should be well-prepared, and he was anxious to combat the system of "trial marriages" popular among the pagans.

Remarkable in that time and place was his insistence that women be treated with respect. Whenever he heard a man refer to his wife by the usual Ibo expression *onye bem*, "the person in my house," Michael would pull him up sharply.

"She is not the person in your house, she is your wife," he would say.

Michael modeled his life on his favorite saint, the Curé of Ars. Traveling to outlying villages on foot, he would spend whole days hearing confessions. He slept little, and fasted frequently, rising to pray at 3 a.m. In Lent he slept on pebbles. His cassocks, though old and patched, were always neat and spotless.

When he didn't travel on foot, he cycled or rode an old motorbike that frequently broke down. Sick calls were answered immediately and without question, and he worked tirelessly during a smallpox epidemic.

Each time he was asked to move to a new post, both he and his parishioners were distressed, but he accepted the transfer without question. Meanwhile, in the long hours he spent before the Blessed Sacrament, the desire grew for the contemplative life. In 1944 he asked Archbishop Heerey of Onitsha for permission to join a monastic order. The archbishop replied that he could not be spared from pastoral work.

He spent four years, from 1945 to 1949, in his parish at Akpu/Ajalli. Here he worked as hard as ever and here, as before, he earned the respect of pagans and Christians alike.

In 1946 a young friend named Stephen Ezeanya wrote from the seminary to say that he was having serious doubts about his vocation. He asked for Michael's advice.

Unusually, Michael took some days to reply to the letter. When the reply did arrive, Stephen was about to tell the rector that he had decided to leave. It said: "Dear Stephen, How do you know that this inclination is not from the devil? If you think you have no vocation, pray for one."

"All my difficulties vanished and never returned," recalled Archbishop Ezeanya years later.

Michael's gift for fostering vocations is possibly the most remarkable feature of his life. Among the many whom he influenced is Cardinal Francis Arinze, now a senior member of the curia. Cardinal Arinze, one of the first children whom Michael baptized, has pointed out that even today, the parishes in which he ministered continue to produce a large number of priests and religious.

In 1949 Archbishop Heerey relented and told Michael that he would help him to become a monk. Realizing the need for contemplative orders in Africa, he hoped that one day Michael would return and help to found a monastery there.

After a pilgrimage to Rome, Michael and the archbishop arrived at Mount Saint Bernard, the Trappist monastery in the English midlands where Michael was to spend the rest of his life. Here he followed the strict rule of those times, which allowed monks to speak only rarely. This must have been hard for a man of his dynamic qualities.

Because there was already a Father Michael in the community, Michael became Father Cyprian. He had never seen snow or ice before, and he suffered greatly during the cold English winters, for the monastery was unheated. Work outdoors was even harder.

"He never complained," recalled a brother monk, Father Anselm. "But when we started to work in the garden, I gave him my donkey jacket. I have never seen anyone more elated or grateful."

Although he never spoke or wrote of his past achievements, he prayed constantly for the people of his homeland. Occasionally he gave retreats to Nigerians visiting the monastery. "Speaking to them he seemed a different man, and had a strong, authoritative voice," observed another monk, Father Paul.

His childlike humility and his unfailing kindness made him greatly loved by the whole community. And he had not forgotten how to laugh.

"He had a great sense of humor and a lovely, deep chuckle," Father Paul remembered. Before flying to Nigeria for the beatification, Father Anselm observed: "Cyprian would be the first to give a deep belly-chuckle if he knew all the fuss being made about him now."

As his reputation for holiness spread to the outside world, increasing numbers of people came to see him, several bishops among them. Although Cyprian left no book, letters and retreat notes contain rich spiritual insights.

Before one retreat he wrote: "One of the sure signs of fervor and progress in religious life is joy and contentment. When we are satisfied with God and with His way of dealing with us, it reflects on the countenance. The face is aglow with joy."

And before another: "We do very little good when we embark on our own. We do much good when we allow God to direct us and direct our enterprises. ... We must learn to avoid worrying ourselves about anything, to leave ourselves, our concerns, in the hands of God; learn to do away with anxieties of all sorts. ... And whilst doing whatever we have to do, we should do it at a pace and a speed that will allow us time continually to turn to God for guidance ... our conversation with God should be continual."

In 1963 the abbot of Mount Saint Bernard decided that Cyprian should return to Africa as novice master of a new monastery in Cameroon, close to the border with Nigeria. It was not to be.

Early in the following year, soon after celebrating his priestly silver jubilee, Cyprian became ill with what was at first thought to be lumbago. In fact it was a thrombosis. When his condition worsened, he was transferred to the hospital at Leicester. There he died on January 20, 1964.

The cause for his beatification was opened in Onitsha on January 20, 1986, the twenty-second anniversary of his death. In September of that year, at the request of Archbishop Ezeanya, his remains were exhumed from the cemetery at Mount Saint Bernard and taken back to Nigeria.

Among those who heard the news of their arrival was Philomena Nnana, a twenty-nine-year-old woman suffering from an apparently terminal stomach cancer in an Onitsha hospital.

"I asked to touch the coffin and it was like a bag of cement on my stomach melted," she said later. "Everything disappeared and I felt well again."

The cure was accepted as a miracle for the beatification. Since then many others, in Nigeria and other lands, believe that Blessed Cyprian has answered their prayers.

15

"IN FIVE HOURS
I SHALL SEE JESUS"

Jacques Fesch

As day dawned over Paris, a slim, dark-haired young man stepped through a doorway into the courtyard of La Santé Prison. Surrounded by guards, hands and feet shackled, he walked to the guillotine erected in a corner of the yard during the night. He was pale but otherwise calm.

On the scaffold, he asked the priest beside him for the crucifix and kissed it. Before the blade fell, he uttered his last words: "Holy Virgin, have pity on me!"

The date: October 1, 1957.

Jacques Fesch, a 27-year-old playboy, was beheaded for the murder of a police officer after a bungled robbery.

Yet many Catholics in France now believe that the killer died a saint. Thirty years after his execution, the archbishop of Paris, Cardinal Jean-Marie Lustiger, signed a decree that may one day see him beatified.

The story begins near the Paris Stock Exchange on February 25, 1954. During the evening rush hour, Jacques arrived with a friend at the office of Alexandre Silberstein, a currency dealer in the Rue Vivienne. On the previous day Jacques had arranged to change two million francs into gold bars.

Silberstein asked his son to bring the gold from the safe. With the young man out of the way, Jacques pulled a revolver from his briefcase, pointed it at Silberstein and demanded the cash from the till. His friend, meanwhile, turned and fled.

As Silberstein tried to reason with him, Jacques hit the dealer twice across the head with the revolver butt. He grabbed three hundred thousand francs and ran.

Once outside, Jacques tried to melt into the crowd on the busy street — but Silberstein recovered quickly. Running from his office, he shouted to passersby that Jacques had robbed him.

Now, with the crowd at his heels, the thief took refuge in a building on Les Grands Boulevards. Minutes later he re-emerged, trying to play the part of an innocent citizen. Immediately someone cried: "That's him!"

By this time Jean Vergne, a 35-year-old police officer, had arrived at the scene. Drawing his revolver, he ordered Jacques to put his hands up. Instead Jacques took his own revolver from his raincoat pocket and fired three times. Vergne, a widower with a four-year-old daughter, was shot through the heart.

Enraged, the crowd chased the killer into the Richelieu-Drouot Metro station. Jacques, still firing, wounded one pursuer in the neck before he was finally surrounded and overcome.

The public was shocked to learn that Vergne's murderer was no common criminal but the son of a wealthy banker, Georges Fesch. Jacques, born April 6, 1930, had idled his way through school, then traveled to Germany with the army. After Jacques completed his service, his father found him a well-paying job at the bank. But Jacques soon tired of it.

Georges Fesch had never taken much interest in his son, who was closer to his mother, Marthe. Eventually, his parents parted.

After his stint at the bank, Jacques had no real occupation. He sailed boats, rode horses, drove fast cars, and hung out with a band, where he tried to learn the trumpet.

In a civil ceremony at age twenty-one, he married Pierrette Polack, a neighbor's daughter who was expecting his child. His anti-Semitic parents were horrified: Pierrette, herself a Catholic, had a Jewish father.

A daughter was born, but Jacques continued to see other women. With one of these he had an illegitimate son, Gérard, whom he abandoned to public care. Soon after this, Jacques and Pierrette separated but remained friends.

Bored and restless, Jacques Fesch now conceived a grand plan. He would buy a boat, sail away to the South Pacific and start a new life. For this, of course, he would need money. He petitioned his parents, but for once, they refused.

Very well, he would get the cash himself. He would rob Alexandre Silberstein.

That his mad scheme might go wrong never seemed to have occurred to Jacques. Sitting in court with a bandaged head, he was defiant. He said he was only sorry he had not carried a submachine gun.

Later, to the chaplain at La Santé Prison, he declared: "I've got no faith. No need to trouble yourself about me."

But Paul Baudet, his defense attorney, was a deeply religious man who had returned to the Catholic Church after many years away from it, and who had, for a time, considered entering a Trappist monastery. Baudet resolved to fight, not only for his client's life, but also for his soul.

At first Jacques viewed the lawyer's efforts with amused disdain. He called him "Pope Paul" and "Torquemada" (after the infamous Spanish inquisitor).

Jacques had another advocate in the tough-minded Dominican chaplain Pere Devoyod, and in Brother Thomas, a young Benedictine who knew Pierrette and wrote regularly from his monastery. Jacques's mother-in-law, Madame Polack, also cared for him as for a son.

From the outset, Jacques had little doubt that he would face the guillotine. Despite his bravado, he was afraid. He was also sick with guilt at the trouble he had brought upon his family.

Yet he remained a skeptic — until the night of February 28, 1955, when he experienced a sudden and dramatic conversion. He wrote an account of it two months before his execution:

"I was in bed, eyes open, really suffering for the first time in my life . . . It was then that a cry burst from my breast, an appeal for help — 'My God!' — and instantly, like a violent wind which passes over without anyone knowing where it comes from, the spirit of the Lord seized me by the throat.

"I had an impression of infinite power and kindness and, from that moment onward, I believed with an unshakeable conviction that has never left me."

Jacques was to spend another two-and-a-half years in prison. During that time he lived a life even more ascetic than the rules demanded. He went to bed at seven each evening, gave up chocolate and cigarettes, and took only a half-hour of exercise each day. To Brother Thomas he wrote: "In prison there are two possible solutions. You can rebel against your situation, or you can regard yourself as a monk."

Though he suffered periods of depression, his fear of death was now supplanted by an even stronger feeling — the fear of dying badly.

Meanwhile, the legal process ground slowly on. More than three years after his crime, Jacques finally came to trial. Baudet argued that the shooting had not been premeditated, but was the act of a frightened man facing a hostile crowd.

Jacques himself now expressed remorse for the murder of Jean Vergne and for the grief he had caused the officer's family. This feeling is also shown movingly in his letters and in the journal, published after his death, that he dedicated to his daughter, Veronique.

Neither Baudet's eloquence nor Jacques's remorse moved the court. At 7:45 p.m. on April 8, 1957, Jacques Fesch was sentenced to death.

Though he continued to live an intense prayer life, Jacques did not find it easy to accept his fate. Because his crime was unpremeditated, he believed that he did not deserve to die. He was tempted to hate those who were sending him to the guillotine, but he overcame the temptation. "May each drop of my blood wipe out a mortal sin," he wrote.

As news of his conversion spread to the outside world, some began to show sympathy for the repentant killer. His final hope lay with the president of France, René Coty, a man known for his humanity. But Coty was under strong police pressure not to show mercy, especially at a time when police officers were being murdered by Algerian terrorists on the streets of French cities.

"Tell your client that he has all my esteem and that I wanted very much to reprieve him," the president told Baudet. "But if I did that, I would put the lives of other police officers in danger." He asked that Jacques accept his death so that officers' lives might be spared.

Coty admitted later that he passed a sleepless night before Jacques was guillotined. As the president lay awake, Jacques wrote in his journal: "The last day of struggle — at this time tomorrow I shall be in heaven! May I die as the Lord wishes me to die . . . Night falls and I feel sad, sad . . . I will meditate on the agony of our Lord in the Garden of Olives, but good Jesus, help me! . . . Only five hours to live! In five hours I shall see Jesus."

Gérard, his abandoned son, was also on his mind. He pleaded that the boy should be well cared for.

When Jacques's journal and letters appeared in print, there was widespread interest in France. Young people, especially, were touched by them.

Those who seek Jacques's beatification point to his mystical experience, his fervent spirituality, his self-conquest, and his victorious battle against the demons of bitterness and despair. But the move to beatify him has created controversy.

"Where are we headed, if we start beatifying criminals?" demanded a police union chief. Another, while accepting Jacques's sincerity, warned that the proposed step might encourage offenders to use conversion as a ploy to avoid punishment. One editorial predicted dryly that Jacques would become the patron saint of gunmen, who would in future pack a votive medal of Saint Jacques along with their Magnum 357s. Vergne's daughter, now a lawyer, has refused to comment publicly, but privately has met with Cardinal Lustiger.

Frequently Jacques is likened to the Good Thief on Calvary. "Nobody is ever lost in God's eyes, even when society has condemned him," Lustiger has said. He wishes to see Jacques beatified "to give great hope to those who despise themselves, who see themselves as irredeemably lost."

16

"WE HAVE A JOB TO DO"

Cardinal Basil Hume

From his desk in London, Cardinal Basil Hume phoned his friend Timothy Wright, abbot at Ampleforth Abbey, Yorkshire.

"Timothy, it's cancer," he said simply.

"Basil, I am so happy for you," Abbot Wright replied. "You are going to heaven."

Announcing that he was suffering from terminal stomach cancer, Basil told his clergy: "I have been given two wonderful graces. First, I have been given time to prepare for a new future. Secondly I find myself — uncharacteristically — calm and at peace." He would, he said, carry on working for as long as possible, and he pleaded: "Above all, no fuss."

While he lived, his wish was respected. But his death on June 17, 1999, brought an outpouring of grief across Britain. Television and radio stations altered their schedules to broadcast memorial programs. Thousands filed past the coffin in the hall adjoining Westminster Cathedral.

Three weeks earlier the dying man had left his hospital bed for Buckingham Palace, where Queen Elizabeth II invested him with the rare Order of Merit. Elizabeth, it was said, spoke of Basil as "my cardinal." Three years after his death, she unveiled a statue of the cardinal in his home city, Newcastle-upon-Tyne.

Early in 1976 the gentle Benedictine monk was plucked from his beloved monastery at Ampleforth to become archbishop of Westminster and leader of the Catholic Church in England and Wales.

167

He had been regarded only as an outside candidate. A newspaper assessment read:

"Much too humble to make known his ability. Could easily be missed."

To be missed would undoubtedly have been Basil's own wish. Unlike his robust predecessor, Cardinal John Heenan, Basil Hume was a diffident figure — tall and distinguished in appearance, certainly, and yet prepared to talk frankly to interviewers about such problems as the loneliness of celibacy.

Erect and silver-haired, his dignified appearance hid a down-to-earth sense of humor. When a priest asked how he would like to be addressed, he replied: "I can cope with just about anything short of 'hey you.'"

Born in Newcastle-upon-Tyne, Basil was the son of Sir William Hume, an eminent physician and a Scots Protestant. His Catholic mother, Marie, was the daughter of a French general. Young George (his baptismal name) grew up equally at home in English and French.

Educated by the Ampleforth Benedictines, he took the name Basil when he joined the monastic community. As a novice he suffered from depression and found consolation in sport, especially in rugby and squash, which he played until late in life.

Soccer was his first love, however. A lifelong Newcastle United supporter, Basil once jokingly suggested that the theme tune from the BBC's *Match of the Day* program should be played at his funeral.

In 1950, after degrees at Oxford and Freiburg, Basil was ordained a priest and returned to Ampleforth to teach languages in the school and theology to young monks. He was elected abbot in 1963.

Not everyone greeted his appointment to Westminster with joy. Critics asked whether a monk who had never run a parish, let alone a diocese, was the right man for the job. Basil was soon to prove himself an inspired choice.

Though barriers were breaking down, English Catholicism in 1976 retained something of the fortress mentality. In some quarters, indeed, Catholics were still regarded with suspicion and hostility.

Writing in the London *Times*, Mary Ann Sieghart declared: "He managed to transform the average Englishman's notion of Catholics. When I was at boarding school in the 1970s, we Catholics were thought exotic at best, odious at worst, lodged only just above Jews in the hierarchy of disfavor. Then the job of Lord Chancellor was still forbidden by law to Catholics, and an unwritten law had ensured that no Catholic became leader of either of the main parties or Speaker of the House of Commons."

Today the leader of the opposition Conservative Party, Iain Duncan Smith, is a Catholic, as is his Liberal counterpart, Charles Kennedy, and Speaker Michael Martin. No eyebrow is raised when Labor Prime Minister Tony Blair, an Anglican, goes to Mass with his Catholic wife, Cherie, and their children.

When Queen Elizabeth attended vespers in Westminster Cathedral to mark its centenary in 1995, it was the first time in more than three hundred years that a British sovereign had been present at a Catholic service. Basil himself described this as the high point of his time at Westminster.

Notwithstanding his Scots-French ancestry, Basil Hume was the archetypal English gentleman: courteous, self-deprecating, and well-spoken.

Yet it was his personal holiness that shone through to all. "He drew people to him by his love of God and his deep feeling for humanity," said Britain's chief rabbi, Jonathan Sacks. "While you were with him, you felt enlarged."

He was also the friend and confidant of three archbishops of Canterbury and, during visits to Moscow, established a strong rapport with Orthodox Patriarch Alexis.

"It has long been my belief that there is an ecumenism of the heart," he wrote to Alexis from his deathbed. "Without the heart being involved, we risk just speaking to each other as institutions and that is not enough."

His heart was equally open to the homeless, especially the youngsters, some of whom spent their days in the shadow of his cathedral. He often stopped for a chat and opened a network of centers for them.

Any troubled person who wrote to him got a personal reply, and he gave generously of his time to both national and international causes. "His diocese is all humanity," commented Sheikh Zaki Badawi, a leader of Britain's Muslim community.

He had a special technique to help visitors who he felt might be overawed by his position. Deliberately, he would leave a button of his cassock undone, or wear his scarlet skullcap slightly askew. "It shows them that I am not perfect," he explained.

The kindly cardinal could also be tough. When parents complained about Opus Dei's recruiting methods, Basil told the movement that no one younger than eighteen should be asked to commit themselves full time, and that no youngster should join without seeking parental advice.

Tact and charm were, however, his usual weapons. More than once he headed off some unwelcome Vatican move with a gentle "that is not the way we do things in England."

He showed his true mettle in battling for Irish people wrongly convicted of terrorism in the United Kingdom. In 1974 the Irish Republican Army had planted bombs in two pubs at Guildford, near London, killing five people and injuring many more. Pub bombings in Birmingham killed twenty-one people and left others with horrific injuries.

Under pressure to get results, police forced three young men and a girl to confess to the Guildford explosions. Gerard Conlon, Paul Hill, Paddy Armstrong, and Carole Richardson were jailed for life.

In a subsequent trial Conlon's father, Giuseppe, his aunt and uncle, Anne and Patrick Maguire, and the Maguires' teenage sons, Vincent and Patrick, were jailed with two others for allegedly making the Guildford bombs. A visit to the Conlons in jail convinced Basil that they were innocent. But his immediate concern was to have the sick Giuseppe freed on health grounds. The release order arrived on the day after Giuseppe's death.

After the Birmingham bombings, six Irishmen had been jailed following confessions that they claimed had been beaten out of them. A self-confessed IRA terrorist told Basil during a prison visit that the six were innocent: The real bombers were safe in Dublin.

The prisoners became known as the Guildford Four, the Maguire Seven and the Birmingham Six. Aided by senior politicians and former judges, Basil campaigned vigorously on their behalf. After fresh court hearings, those still in jail were released.

Though politically astute, Basil was totally without guile. His Benedictine colleague, Archbishop Rembert Weakland of Milwaukee, commented: "We have an expression in America that goes, 'What you see is what you get.' In Basil's case one was conscious of a transparency of character, so that the exterior actions and words revealed the interior intellectual and spiritual workings. One never had to second-guess Basil's mind or intent. I never had to wonder what he really meant or to guess if there was some subtle unrevealed motive in his speaking."

Inevitably, Basil Hume had his critics. He was variously accused of being both too conservative and too liberal. To a TV interviewer he explained his position simply: "The pope is the boss and I will obey even if I disagree."

He wrote several books, including *Searching for God* and *To Be a Pilgrim*. The titles are significant. For him the Church was a pilgrim Church, and the life of the Christian a pilgrimage.

"The pilgrim limps along the road," he said. "The pilgrim is always in search and that can be painful."

Again and again he urged perseverance in prayer, even in periods of darkness and discouragement.

On the day of his funeral, Basil was to have spoken to the Washington Theological Union. Archbishop Oscar Lipscomb of Mobile read his address for him.

It urged that contentious issues should not divide the Catholic community or distract believers from their relationship with Christ. Endless controversy, he suggested, might be a trick of the devil to divert Catholics from their essential role — mission.

"The Church does not exist for its own sake," he declared. "We have a job to do."

17

"A LIFE LIVED IN THE FULL SENSE OF THE WORD"

Blessed Luigi Beltrame Quattrocchi and Blessed Maria Corsini

Over the centuries, the Church has canonized or beatified a number of married people, but only once in its entire history has a pope declared a married couple "blessed." On October 21, 2001, Pope John Paul II beatified Luigi Beltrame Quattrocchi and his wife, Maria Corsini. Three of their four children were present at the ceremony.

On that Sunday morning in Saint Peter's, the pope fulfilled a desire that he had expressed over many years: to recognize, by beatifying a husband and wife, the holiness men and women can and do achieve through the vocation of Christian marriage.

Luigi and Maria lived most of their lives in Rome during the first half of the twentieth century. Luigi, born in Catania and raised in Urbino, was adopted at the age of nine by a childless uncle and aunt, from whom he received his second surname. A year later, in 1890, his uncle, a senior customs official, was transferred to the capital. Maria was born in Florence to the noble Corsini family in 1884; she, too, was brought to Rome as a child because of her father's work.

The pair met in 1901, when Luigi was twenty-one and Maria seventeen. He was about to qualify as an attorney, and she was a student at a business college. They married in the Basilica of Saint Mary Major on November 25, 1905.

Though he was honest, hardworking, and unselfish, Luigi did not have a strong faith until he fell in love with Maria, who was devout from early childhood — a cultured girl, fond especially of literature and music. Now Mass and Holy Communion became the center of his life, too, and they recited the Rosary together every day.

In a highly successful career, Luigi held a number of government legal posts and went on to sit on the boards of several banks, including the Bank of Italy. He played an important role in the reconstruction of his country after the war and was a friend of such political figures as Father Luigi Sturzo, Alcide de Gasperi, and Luigi Gedda. He retired as an honorary deputy attorney general of the Italian State.

Maria, a devoted wife and mother, also had a successful career, as a teacher and writer on educational topics. She helped to found the Catholic University of the Sacred Heart and played leading roles in a number of other Catholic organizations, serving on the general council of the Italian Catholic Women's Association. In the 1930s she took a nursing course and worked as a volunteer for the Red Cross during the war in Ethiopia and World War II.

During the Nazi occupation of Rome, the Beltrame family's apartment on Via Depretis, near Saint Mary Major, was a shelter for refugees, some of them Jewish. Nobody who knocked at their door, seeking help of any kind, was ever turned away.

With Luigi, Maria accompanied sick pilgrims to Lourdes as a volunteer helper. Together the couple founded a scout group for youngsters in a poor part of Rome.

Of the couple's four children, two became priests and one a nun. Father Tarcisio, the eldest, is a priest of the Rome diocese; Stefania, who entered the Benedictine order and took the name Cecilia, died in 1993; Cesare became a Trappist monk and is now Father Paolino; the youngest child, Enrichetta, stayed at home to look after her parents.

With Enrichetta the pregnancy was difficult, with the lives of mother and baby both apparently in danger. One of Rome's leading gynecologists advised an abortion to try to save Maria's life. He bluntly told Luigi that there was only a five percent chance that she and the baby would survive, and asked how he would face the prospect of bringing up three children on his own.

Of course, for Luigi and Maria an abortion was unthinkable. They put their trust in God, and Enrichetta was born safely. At the age of eighty-seven she attended her parents' beatification together with her two brothers, both in their nineties.

It was not simply for their apostolic work, or because they gave three children to the Church, that the couple were beatified. These were simply the fruits of the deep spirituality with which they lived their married life.

Their home was consecrated to the Sacred Heart of Jesus, whose image was placed on the mantelpiece of their dining room. They kept the family holy hour on the first Friday of every month, went on weekend retreats organized by the Benedictines at Saint Paul-Outside-The-Walls, and took graduate religious courses at the Gregorian University.

Both Franciscan tertiaries, they joyfully encouraged their children's vocations to the priesthood and the religious life, and would have offered Enrichetta equally gladly, had this been asked of them. After twenty years of marriage, under the guidance of their spiritual director, the couple took a vow to renounce marital relations in order to be able to respond totally to any call from God.

Maria described their daily routine. "The day began like this: Mass and Communion, together. Once we were out of the church he would say 'good morning' to me, as if the day began only then. We would buy the newspaper, then go back to the house. He would go to work, I would go about my various tasks. Each of us fulfilling our responsibilities, but keeping a sense of the other's presence constantly within us."

Of the evenings, she wrote: "Dinner, some passages from good books, then the Rosary. A life serene, intellectual, interesting, intimate, and restful. Never futile, never sad or pessimistic. A life lived in the full sense of the word. Not hurried, but enlivened by a sense of fulfillment at every moment, with the joy of being together, always new."

Friends visited constantly, and there were holidays, with walking and cycling trips in the mountains.

Cardinal José Martins, prefect of the Congregation for the Causes of Saints, said that the couple "made a true domestic church of their family, which was open to life, to prayer, to the social apostolate, to solidarity with the poor and to friendship."

Luigi died of a heart attack at home in Rome on November 9, 1951. Maria died in Enrichetta's arms at their holiday cottage in the mountains at Serravalle on August 25, 1965.

Their beatification cause went forward when Gilberto Grossi, a young Italian, was cured after praying to them. He had been suffering from a severe form of arthritis that frequently confined him to bed and from a progressive intestinal inflammation that caused external ulcers. His cure, which doctors found beyond scientific explanation, was accepted as miraculous. Today Dr. Grossi is a neurosurgeon.

At the beatification ceremony, Pope John Paul told the three Beltrame children: "Dear friends, this is what your mother wrote about you: 'We brought them up in the faith, so that they might know and love God.'

"But your parents also handed on the burning lamp to their friends, acquaintances, colleagues.... And now, from heaven, they are giving it to the whole Church."

18

"I AM THE HAPPIEST MAN ON THE FACE OF THE EARTH"

Father Mychal Judge, O.F.M.

On the day after the terrorist attack of September 11, 2001, newspapers across the world ran a picture of rescue workers carrying the lifeless body of a Catholic priest from the ruins of the World Trade Center.

Father Mychal Judge, a sixty-eight-year-old Franciscan, was killed by falling debris as he ministered to the dead and dying at the foot of the collapsing Tower One. Father Mychal, a chaplain to the New York City Fire Department, went to the scene as soon as he got news of the attack. Entering the stricken building with a squad of firemen, he passed Mayor Rudolph Giuliani, who asked him: "Please pray for us."

"I always do," Father Mychal called back, as he hurried toward his death.

A widely published account says that the chaplain was hit by debris after removing his helmet to give last rites to a senior fire officer who had himself been killed by the falling body of a woman who had jumped from the tower. The story may not be strictly accurate, but that scarcely matters. He died a hero and, in the eyes of many who knew him, he also died a saint.

A priest of charismatic personality, Mychal Judge was a familiar figure on the streets of Manhattan in his brown Franciscan habit. His countless friends included a former president of the United States and AIDS victims abandoned even by those closest to them. Because he presented a joyful face to the world, few knew of the hard battle he had fought against his own inner demons.

Born in Brooklyn on May 11, 1933, Emmet Judge was the son of two Irish immigrants from County Leitrim who met on the voyage to New York. His father died after a long illness when Emmet was only six. To help his mother and two sisters make ends meet, he shined shoes at Pennsylvania Station, ran errands, and did odd jobs.

Of his father's death, he said later: "When tragedy strikes us at an early age, maybe religion takes on a greater meaning. The closer tragedy is to our heart and home, the more likely faith is to form, because we have been tested and tried, and from that comes faith."

His shoe-shine stand was close to Saint Francis of Assisi Church on West 31st Street, where the fatherless young boy in time felt the first stirrings of his own Franciscan vocation. He entered the order in 1954, made his final profession in 1958 and was ordained in 1961. In religion he took the name Mychal, though to many of his friends, and especially to the firemen, he was known simply as "Father Mike."

A fellow priest recalled that his first assignment was to a parish where the pastor was inclined to handle people roughly. "He would hear the pastor yelling at people who had come in for counseling, wait for them to come out and take them to another room, to smooth them over and assure them that God loved them," he said.

Mychal himself once told a journalist: "In seminary you get all the theology and Scripture in the world, and you land in your first parish and you find out it's you — your personality and the gifts that God gave you."

Most of his early years as a priest were spent in New Jersey parishes, though he also served for a time as assistant to the president at Siena College in Loudonville, New York. During his five years as pastor at Saint Joseph's in West Milford, a series of tragedies hit families in the town. No fewer than five teenagers committed suicide, and several more died in alcohol-related automobile accidents.

His reflection on those troubled times came echoing back in the wake of the terrorist attack in which he died. "There are really no answers that you can give to people," he said, "but somehow you have to give them the eternal vision of God."

Fellow Franciscans testified to his success. "He was here at such a trying time for this community," said Father Bernard Splawaski, "and he managed to give hope to so many people."

On one occasion he was called to a house where a distraught man was holding his wife and children at gunpoint on the upper floor. Hitching his habit so that he would not trip, Mychal climbed a ladder and told the man gently: "We can talk this over. We can go have a cup of coffee. This isn't the way to handle things."

The watchers below dreaded hearing a gunshot, but it didn't happen. The man laid the gun aside, and nobody was hurt. If Mychal realized the danger he was in, he never showed it.

As a boy he had dreamed of becoming a firefighter, and his fascination with their world never left him. In New Jersey he became a familiar figure at firemen's celebrations, and at the funerals of the fallen and the bedsides of the injured.

In 1986, after a period of study in England, Mychal was assigned to Saint Francis of Assisi in Manhattan, the church that he knew so well in his shoe-shining days. He was soon called to Bellevue Hospital to say Mass for Steven McDonald, a police officer paralyzed from the neck down after being shot by a fifteen-year-old boy he was questioning in Central Park.

"He was in bad shape, but determined to live," Mychal observed afterward.

In the following years Mychal became very close to McDonald and his wife and son, traveling with them on speaking tours in the United States and Northern Ireland.

"He was my confessor, spiritual advisor, and my best friend," said McDonald. "He was my idea of what a priest should be and, above all, he was a living example of Jesus Christ."

Mychal's appointment as firefighters' chaplain in 1992 was a dream come true. "I always wanted to become a priest or a firefighter; now I'm both," he told friends.

He often took his meals at the firehouse across the road from his home in the friary and called the firemen "my boys." As in his New Jersey days, he sometimes had to conduct the funerals of men killed on duty, and to comfort their families afterward.

Yet his ministry extended much further. Crime victims, the homeless, AIDS sufferers, alcoholics, and the gay community — all found a friend in the gray-haired Franciscan with the big Irish smile.

To those with a drinking problem he would say: "You're not a bad person — you have a disease that makes you think you're a bad person, and it's going to foul you up." He spoke from the heart, for he himself had for a time fallen victim to alcoholism, and the day of his funeral was the twenty-third anniversary of his liberation.

Each year his recovering alcoholic friends got a note on their own "date of sobriety." He once told President Clinton at the White House that Alcoholics Anonymous was America's greatest contribution to spirituality.

He took up the case of a priest falsely accused of an offense against a minor, flying to Ireland to assure the accused man's superior that he was totally innocent. As a result, the priest was defended by a top New York attorney and an angry judge threw out the case.

Mychal cared for AIDS victims at a time when others shunned them. He once bent to kiss the forehead of a man dying alone in conditions of squalor. "You know, no one touches him," he said. "He must feel so lonely."

A close friend, Franciscan Father Michael Duffy, recalled: "Even though a person might approach him as pastor, chaplain, whatever, within thirty seconds all of those titles fell down and he was just a friend."

To people in Manhattan he seemed to have the gift of being everywhere at once. On an ordinary day, he would receive as many as forty phone messages on his answering machine. "He seemed to know everybody in the world," said Father Duffy.

"Countless people told me that on birthdays, anniversaries, dates of sobriety — whatever — they would get a little note from him. He must have kept a huge calendar! In everyone's lives, whatever was significant, he'd write them a little note about it or give them a telephone call. Everyone considered him family."

When TWA Flight 800 crashed into the sea off Long Island in 1996 with the loss of all two hundred thirty people on board, Mychal drove to the hotel near JFK Airport where the bereaved families gathered. For more than two weeks he spent twelve hours a day there, consoling all who had lost loved ones, regardless of their religion. He said Mass and organized ecumenical services for the bereaved and for TWA staff.

"The TWA families considered him a saint," said a spokesman. Each year, on the anniversary of the crash, Mychal helped to organize services on the beach close to the site. After the service in 2000, newspapers across the United States carried a picture of him, dressed in his Franciscan habit and gazing out to sea.

Although he saw so much trouble and tragedy, Mychal never lost his sense of fun. He loved to tell jokes and stories, to sing Irish songs, and he was not above the odd act of mischief. On one occasion, at a White House reception, he hid a handful of monogrammed cocktail napkins in his habit and distributed them as presents to his friends.

Former President Clinton, Senator Hillary Clinton, and their daughter, Chelsea, were present at Mychal's funeral Mass in Saint Francis of Assisi Church, where Cardinal Edward Egan presided.

Mychal Judge lived his Franciscan poverty to the full, sleeping on a sofa bed in his sparsely furnished room at the friary. Yet he felt himself to be richer than any millionaire.

Preaching the homily, Father Michael Duffy recalled how his friend would recount one by one the blessings God had given him, and for which he was constantly grateful; chief among them his family, his friends, and his Franciscan priesthood.

"Do you know what I want?" he asked once.

"No, Mike, what do you want?" his friend responded.

"Nothing — absolutely nothing," Mychal told him. "I am the happiest man on the face of the earth."

Bibliography

Franz Jägerstätter

Kent, Bruce. *Franz Jägerstätter*. London: Catholic Truth Society, 1976.

Zahn, Gordon C. *In Solitary Witness*. Austin, Texas: Holt, Rinehart & Winston, 1964.

John Bradburne

Crystal, David, ed. *Songs of the Vagabond*. Leominster, UK: Holy Island Press, 1996.

Dove, John, S.J. *Strange Vagabond of God*. London: Gracewing, 1997.

Moore, Charles. "A Holy Man in Africa," *Catholic Herald* (November 28, 1997).

Venerable Marthe Robin

Peyret, R. *Prends ma Vie, Seigneur: La Longue Messe de Marthe Robin*. Paris: Desclee de Brower, 1985.

Peyret, R. *Marthe Robin: The Cross and the Joy*. New York: Alba House, 1983.

Tierney, Michel; Martin Blake; and David Fanning. *Marthe Robin, A Chosen Soul*. London: Catholic Truth Society, 1999.

Venerable Edel Quinn

Ball, Ann. *Modern Saints, Their Lives and Faces, Book Two*. Rockford, Ill.: Tan Books, 1990.

Suenens, L-J. *Edel Quinn*. Dublin: Fallon, 1954.

Father Vincent McNabb, O.P.

Siderman, E.A. *A Saint in Hyde Park*. London: Geoffrey Bles, 1950.

Valentine, Ferdinand, O.P. *Father Vincent McNabb, O.P.* London: Burns and Oates, 1955.

Dr. Tom Dooley

Dooley, Agnes W. *Promises to Keep*. New York: Farrar, Strauss, and Cudahy, 1961.

Dooley, Thomas A. *Deliver Us from Evil*. New York: Farrar, Strauss, and Cudahy, 1958.

Dooley, Thomas A. *The Night They Burned the Mountain*. New York: Farrar, Strauss, and Cudahy, 1960.

Monahan, James. *Before I Sleep*. New York: Farrar, Strauss, and Cudahy, 1961.

Venerable Matt Talbot

Ball, Ann. *Modern Saints, Their Lives and Faces, Book Two*. Rockford, Ill.: Tan Books, 1990.

Doherty, Eddie. *Matt Talbot*. Milwaukee: Bruce Publishing Co., 1953.

Purcell, Mary. *Matt Talbot and His Times*. Chicago: Franciscan Herald Press, 1977.

Blessed Brother André

Ball, Ann. *Modern Saints, Their Lives and Faces*. Rockford, Ill.: Tan Books, 1983.

Burton, Katherine. *Brother André of Mount Royal*. Dublin: Clontarf and Reynolds, 1955.

Venerable Charles de Foucauld

Gorrée, Georges. *Memories of Charles de Foucauld*. London: Burns, Oates, and Washbourne, 1938.

Hamilton, Elizabeth. *The Desert My Dwelling Place*. London: Hodder and Stoughton, 1968.

Little Brother of Jesus, A. *Pilgrimage to God: The Spirit of Charles de Foucauld*. London: Darton, Longman, and Todd, 1974.

Trouncer, Margaret. *Charles de Foucauld*. London: Harrap, 1972.

Saint Edith Stein

Ball, Ann. *Modern Saints, Their Lives and Faces*. Rockford, Ill.: Tan Books, 1983.

de Fabregues, Jean. *Edith Stein*. New York: Alba House, 1965.

Graef, Hilda C. *The Scholar and the Cross*. London: Longmans Green, 1955.

Oesterreicher, John M. *Walls Are Crumbling*. London: Hollis and Carter, 1953.

Pope John Paul I

Cornwell, John. *A Thief in the Night*. New York: Penguin Putnam, 2001.

Tierney, Dr. M.A. *Pope John Paul I (Albino Luciani) 1912-1978*. e-book: drmat@indigo.ie

Saint Josephine Bakhita

Ball, Ann. *Modern Saints, Their Lives and Faces, Book Two*. Rockford, Ill.: Tan Books, 1990.

Roche, Aloysius. *Bakhita, Pearl of the Sudan*. Langley, Buckinghamshire, UK: Saint Paul Publications, 1968.

Archbishop Oscar Romero

Brockman, James R., S.J. *Romero: A Life*. Maryknoll, N.Y.: Orbis Books, 1989.

Sobrino, Jon, S.J. *Archbishop Romero, Memories and Reflections*. Maryknoll, N.Y.: Orbis Books, 1990.

Vigil, Maria Lopez. *Oscar Romero: Memories in Mosaic*. Washington, D.C.: EPICA, 2000.

Blessed Cyprian Tansi

Isichei, Elizabeth. *Entirely For God*. Spencer, Mass.: Cistercian Publications, 1999.

Kogbara, Donu. "The Miracle Worker," (London) *Daily Mail* (March 23, 1998).

Jacques Fesch

Ball, Ann. *Faces of Holiness II*. Huntington, Ind.: Our Sunday Visitor, 2001.

Duchesne, Jean and Bernard Gouley. *L'Affaire Jacques Fesch*. Paris: Editions du Fallois, 1994.

Fesch, Jacques. *Light Over the Scaffold: The Prison Letters of Jacques Fesch*. New York: Alba House, 1998.

Cardinal Basil Hume

Butler, Carolyn, ed. *Basil Hume: By His Friends*. London: Fount Paperbacks, 1999.

Stanford, Peter. *Cardinal Basil Hume*. London: Geoffrey Chapman, 1993.

Blessed Luigi Beltrame Quattrocchi and Blessed Maria Corsini

"Blessed Luigi Beltrame Quattrocchi (1880-1951) and Blessed Maria Corsini (1884-1965)," *L'Osservatore Romano Weekly English Edition* (October 10, 2001).

Joustrate, Bernard. "Les Bienheureux Luigi et Maria Quattrocchi," *Tradinews* (http://perso.club-internet.fr/xgarnaud/BxEpouxQuattrocchi.html).

"Fondazione Luigi e Maria Quattrocchi" (www2.glauco.it/fondazionebq/luigi.htm).

Father Mychal Judge, O.F.M.

Feister, John Bookser and John Zawadzinski. "No Greater Love: Chaplain Mychal Judge, O.F.M." *Saint Anthony Messenger* (December 2001).

Senior, Jennifer. "The Firemen's Friar," *New York Metro* (December 1, 2001).

Alonso-Aldivar, Ricardo. "His Parish Knew No Bounds," *L.A. Times* (September 16, 2001).

"For Whom the Bell Tolls," *The* (New York) *Village Voice* (September 19-25, 2001).

IF YOU COULD LOOK INTO THE FACE OF HOLINESS,
WHAT WOULD YOU SEE?

Faces of Holiness and **Faces of Holiness II,** by Ann Ball, capture a glimpse of the lives of numerous contemporary martyrs and saints, making their stories real through personal accounts and photos. These accounts of humanity and holiness can give hope to us all.

Faces of Holiness
by Ann Ball
0-87973-950-9, (950)
paper, 272 pp.

Faces of Holiness II
by Ann Ball
0-87973-409-4, (409)
paper, 272 pp.

Our Sunday Visitor ...

YOUR SOURCE FOR DISCOVERING THE RICHES
OF THE CATHOLIC FAITH

Our Sunday Visitor has an extensive line of materials for young children, teens, and adults. Our books, Bibles, booklets, CD-ROMs, and audio and video products are available in bookstores worldwide.

To receive a FREE full-line catalog or for more information, call Our Sunday Visitor at 1-800-348-2440. Or write Our Sunday Visitor / 200 Noll Plaza / Huntington, IN 46750.

• •

____ **Please send me a catalog.**
Please send me materials on:
____ Apologetics and catechetics   ____ Reference works
____ Prayer books   ____ Heritage and the saints
____ The family   ____ The parish

Name: _____

Address: _____ Apt.: _____

City: _____ State: ____ ZIP: _____

Telephone: ( ) _____ A29BBABP

• •

____ Please send a friend a catalog.
Please send a friend materials on:
____ Apologetics and catechetics   ____ Reference works
____ Prayer books   ____ Heritage and the saints
____ The family   ____ The parish

Name: _____

Address: _____ Apt.: _____

City: _____ State: _____ ZIP: _____

Telephone: ( ) _____ A29BBABP

• •

OurSundayVisitor

200 Noll Plaza / Huntington, IN 46750 / 1-800-348-2440 / osvbooks@osv.com / www.osv.com